First World War
and Army of Occupation
War Diary
France, Belgium and Germany

50 DIVISION
150 Infantry Brigade
Durham Light Infantry
1/5th Battalion
23 January 1914 - 31 January 1918

WO95/2837/2

The Naval & Military Press Ltd
www.nmarchive.com
Published in association with The National Archives

Published by

The Naval & Military Press Ltd

Unit 10 Ridgewood Industrial Park,

Uckfield, East Sussex,

TN22 5QE England

Tel: +44 (0) 1825 749494

www.naval-military-press.com

www.nmarchive.com

This diary has been reprinted in facsimile from the original. Any imperfections are inevitably reproduced and the quality may fall short of modern type and cartographic standards.

© **Crown Copyright**
Images reproduced by permission of The National Archives, London, England, 2015.

Contents

Document type	Place/Title	Date From	Date To
Heading	50th Division 150th Infy Bde 5th Bn Durham Lt Infy 1914 Jly-Jan 1918		
Heading	5th Durham L. Inf 1914 Jly-1915 Apl		
Heading	War Diary 5th Bn. Durham L. Infy 29th July 1914 To 30th July 1915		
War Diary	Deqaucoy	29/07/1914	29/07/1914
War Diary	Stockton	30/07/1914	30/07/1914
War Diary	Deqaucoy	03/08/1914	03/08/1914
War Diary	Stockton	04/08/1914	05/08/1914
War Diary	South Gare	06/08/1914	10/08/1914
War Diary	West Hartlepool & Hartlepool	06/08/1914	08/08/1914
War Diary	Hartlepool	09/08/1914	05/09/1914
War Diary	Darlington	06/09/1914	16/10/1914
War Diary	Newcastle	17/10/1914	31/12/1914
War Diary	Hurworth	01/01/1915	22/01/1915
War Diary	Newcastle	23/01/1914	14/04/1914
War Diary	Deqaucoy	29/07/1914	29/07/1914
War Diary	Stockton	30/07/1914	30/07/1914
War Diary	Deqaucoy	03/08/1914	03/08/1914
War Diary	Stockton	04/08/1914	05/08/1914
War Diary	South Gare	06/08/1914	10/08/1914
War Diary	West Hartlepool & Hartlepool	06/08/1914	08/08/1914
War Diary	Hartlepool	09/08/1914	05/09/1914
War Diary	Darlington	06/09/1914	16/10/1914
War Diary	Newcastle	17/10/1914	31/12/1914
War Diary	Hurworth	01/01/1915	22/01/1915
War Diary	Newcastle	23/01/1915	29/03/1915
Heading	150th Inf. Bde 50th Div War Diary 1/5th Battn The Durham Light Infantry April 1915		
War Diary	Newcastle	01/04/1915	16/04/1915
War Diary	Boulogne	17/04/1915	18/04/1915
War Diary	Steeinvoord	19/04/1915	25/04/1915
War Diary	St. Julien	26/04/1915	28/04/1915
War Diary	Rest Camp Near Brierlen	29/04/1915	29/04/1915
War Diary	Brierlen	30/04/1915	30/04/1915
Heading	150th Inf. Bde 50th Div 1/5th Battn. The Durham Light Infantry May 1915		
War Diary		01/05/1915	01/05/1915
War Diary	Near Popperinghe	02/05/1915	02/05/1915
War Diary	Steinvoorde	03/05/1915	03/05/1915
War Diary	St. Laurent	04/05/1915	11/05/1915
War Diary	Hoogu	12/05/1915	26/05/1915
War Diary	C Camp	26/05/1915	28/05/1915
War Diary	Bunt Camp Vlamertinghe	29/05/1915	29/05/1915
Heading	150th Inf Bde 50th Div 1/5th Battn. The Durham Light Infantry June 1915		
War Diary	B Camp Vlamertinghe	04/06/1915	24/06/1915
War Diary	Dettingen Huts	25/06/1915	30/06/1915
Heading	150th Inf. Bde 50th Div. 1/5th Battn. The Durham Light Infantry July 1915		

War Diary		01/07/1915	09/07/1915
War Diary	Dettingen Huts Dranoutre	10/07/1915	17/07/1915
War Diary	Armentieres	21/07/1915	24/07/1915
War Diary	L. Epinette	30/07/1915	30/07/1915
Heading	150th Inf. Bde. 50th Div. 1/5th Battn. The Durham Light Infantry. August 1915		
Miscellaneous	1/5th Battalion The Durham Light Infantry August 1915		
War Diary	L'Epinnette Trenches	01/08/1915	04/08/1915
War Diary	Armentieres	07/08/1915	20/08/1915
War Diary	Trenches 67 & 68 Chapelle Armentieres	20/08/1915	25/08/1915
War Diary	Armentieres	26/08/1915	31/08/1915
Heading	150th Inf. Bde 50th Div. 1/5th Battn. The Durham Light Infantry September 1915		
War Diary	Asylum Armentieres	01/09/1915	12/09/1915
War Diary	Armentieres	12/09/1915	18/09/1915
War Diary	Trenches	19/09/1915	26/09/1915
War Diary	Trenches 72 & 73	26/09/1915	29/09/1915
Heading	150th Inf. Bde. 50th Div 1/5th Battn. The Durham Light Infantry October 1915		
War Diary		03/10/1915	04/10/1915
War Diary	Asylum	05/10/1915	05/10/1915
War Diary	Armentieres	05/10/1915	06/10/1915
War Diary	Trenches 67 & 68	07/10/1915	14/10/1915
War Diary	Armentieres	15/10/1915	15/10/1915
War Diary	Trenches 71-73	16/10/1915	22/10/1915
War Diary	Armentieres	23/10/1915	31/10/1915
Heading	150th Inf. Bde. 50th Div. 1/5th Battn. The Durham Light Infantry November 1915		
War Diary	Armentieres	01/11/1915	17/11/1915
War Diary	Oultersteen	19/11/1915	30/11/1915
Heading	150th Inf. Bde. 50th Div. 1/5th Battn. The Durham Light Infantry December 1915		
War Diary	Outtersteene	01/12/1915	20/12/1915
War Diary	Dickebush Huts	21/12/1915	23/12/1915
War Diary	Trenches A3-A6	24/12/1915	27/12/1915
War Diary	Armagh Wood	24/12/1915	27/12/1915
War Diary	Ypres	24/12/1915	27/12/1915
War Diary	Railway Dug Outs 1.20.d.6.8	24/12/1915	31/12/1915
War Diary	Trenches A3-A6	31/12/1915	31/12/1915
Heading	1/5th Durham L.I. Jan Vol VII		
War Diary	Trenches A3-A6	01/01/1916	01/01/1916
War Diary	Armagh Wood	01/01/1916	01/01/1916
War Diary	Dickebush Huts	04/01/1916	06/01/1916
War Diary	Trenches A3-A6	07/01/1916	07/01/1916
War Diary	Railway Dug Outs	11/01/1916	11/01/1916
War Diary	Trenches A3-A6 RI	15/01/1916	26/01/1916
War Diary	Armagh Wood	27/01/1916	31/01/1916
War Diary	Scottish Lines	01/02/1916	01/02/1916
War Diary	Busseboom	02/02/1916	06/02/1916
War Diary	Hill 60	06/02/1916	06/02/1916
War Diary	Trenches 37c To 48 R Hill 60	07/02/1916	13/02/1916
War Diary	Bedford House I.26.A.8.1.	13/02/1916	18/02/1916
War Diary	Scottish Lines	19/02/1916	19/02/1916
War Diary	Busseboom H. 23. B. 5.9	20/02/1916	21/02/1916
War Diary	Scottish Lines	22/02/1916	24/02/1916
War Diary	Trenches A.4-A.11	25/02/1916	25/02/1916

War Diary	Ypres	25/02/1916	27/02/1916
War Diary	Trenches A.9-A.12	27/02/1916	01/03/1916
War Diary	Sanctuary Wood	01/03/1916	12/03/1916
War Diary	Popperinghe	13/03/1916	14/03/1916
War Diary	Dickebush Huts. A.	15/03/1916	17/03/1916
War Diary	Hill.60.	18/03/1916	18/03/1916
War Diary	Trenches 37 To 40	18/03/1916	18/03/1916
War Diary	Hill 60	24/03/1916	24/03/1916
War Diary	Scottish Lines	25/03/1916	31/03/1916
War Diary	Busseboom	26/03/1916	31/03/1916
Heading	1/5 Durham L.I. Vol X.		
War Diary	Badajos Huts Locre	01/04/1916	02/04/1916
War Diary	G1-H1A Trenches At Kemmel Centre Brigade Left Sub Sector	07/04/1916	07/04/1916
War Diary	Trenches G1-H1A Kemmel	12/04/1916	14/04/1916
War Diary	Kemmel Shelters	15/04/1916	22/04/1916
War Diary	Trenches G1-H1A	22/04/1916	28/04/1916
War Diary	Locre	28/04/1916	28/04/1916
War Diary	Caestre	29/04/1916	24/05/1916
War Diary	Trenches G1-H1A Kemmel	01/06/1916	14/06/1916
War Diary	Locre	15/06/1916	17/06/1916
War Diary	Kemmel Shelters	28/06/1916	31/06/1916
War Diary	Locre	19/06/1916	19/06/1916
War Diary	Camp La. Clytte	20/06/1916	30/06/1916
Heading	War Diary 5th Bn Durham L.I. July 1916 Volume 16		
War Diary	La. Clytte Camp	01/07/1916	04/07/1916
War Diary	Trenches K 2 A To L 7	05/07/1916	15/07/1916
War Diary	R.C Farm	16/07/1916	16/07/1916
War Diary	Trenches G1 To H2	19/07/1916	19/07/1916
War Diary	Kemmel Shelters	22/07/1916	24/07/1916
War Diary	Trenches K 2A To L 7	25/07/1916	31/07/1916
War Diary	R.C. Farm	31/07/1916	31/07/1916
War Diary	Kemmel	01/08/1916	04/08/1916
War Diary	Locre	07/08/1916	08/08/1916
War Diary	Caestre	08/08/1916	09/08/1916
War Diary	Autheux	11/08/1916	11/08/1916
War Diary	Villers Bocage	15/08/1916	15/08/1916
War Diary	Molliens-Au-Bois	16/08/1916	16/08/1916
War Diary	Kemmel	01/08/1916	04/08/1916
War Diary	Locre	07/08/1916	08/08/1916
War Diary	Caestre	08/08/1916	09/08/1916
War Diary	Autheux	11/08/1916	11/08/1916
War Diary	Villers Bocage	15/08/1916	15/08/1916
War Diary	Molliens-Au-Bois	16/08/1916	16/08/1916
War Diary	Molliens	17/08/1916	17/08/1916
War Diary	Millencourt	18/08/1916	31/08/1916
War Diary	Molliens	17/08/1916	17/08/1916
War Diary	Millencourt	18/08/1916	31/08/1916
Heading	150th Infantry Brigade 50th Division 5th Durham Light Infantry 150th Infantry Brigade September 1916		
War Diary	Millencourt	01/09/1916	14/09/1916
War Diary	Bezantin-Le-Petit	15/09/1916	27/09/1916
War Diary	O.G.1. Bezantin-Le-Petit	28/09/1916	29/09/1916
War Diary	Mametz Wood	30/09/1916	30/09/1916
Heading	5th Battalion The Durham Light Infantry October 1916 Vol XIX		

War Diary	Mametz Wood	01/10/1916	01/10/1916
War Diary	O.G.1	02/10/1916	02/10/1916
War Diary	Mametz Wood	03/10/1916	03/10/1916
War Diary	Albert	04/10/1916	04/10/1916
War Diary	Baizieux Wood	05/10/1916	23/10/1916
War Diary	Millencourt	24/10/1916	24/10/1916
War Diary	Bazentin	25/10/1916	27/10/1916
War Diary	Bazentin Le Grand	28/10/1916	28/10/1916
War Diary	Le Trenches	29/10/1916	31/10/1916
War Diary	Flers Line Trenches	01/11/1916	02/11/1916
War Diary	Bazentin Le Grand	02/11/1916	02/11/1916
War Diary	Mametz	03/11/1916	05/11/1916
War Diary	Trenches	06/11/1916	11/11/1916
War Diary	Bazentin Le Grand	16/11/1916	16/11/1916
War Diary	Becourt	17/11/1916	29/11/1916
War Diary	Baizieux	30/11/1916	30/11/1916
Miscellaneous	Volume 20		
War Diary	Baizieux	01/12/1916	30/12/1916
War Diary	Albert	31/12/1916	31/12/1916
Heading	Volume 21		
War Diary	Albert	01/01/1917	01/01/1917
War Diary	Bazentin Le Petit	07/01/1917	08/01/1917
War Diary	Trenches Durham Road	09/01/1917	12/01/1917
War Diary	Trenches	15/01/1917	16/01/1917
War Diary	Bazentin Le Petit	22/01/1917	28/01/1917
War Diary	Fricourt	28/01/1917	28/01/1917
War Diary	Buire	30/01/1917	31/01/1917
Heading	5 Batt Durham Light Infantry Volume 22 January 1917		
Heading	Headquarters 150 Infantry Bde Attached Is War Diary For Month Of February 1917		
War Diary	Buire	01/02/1917	08/02/1917
War Diary	Morcourt	09/02/1917	10/02/1917
War Diary	Foucaucourt	11/02/1917	15/02/1917
Heading	5 Bn Durham Light Infantry Volume 23 February		
War Diary	Foucacourt	15/02/1917	16/02/1917
War Diary	La Trenches	20/02/1917	20/02/1917
War Diary	Foucacourt	20/02/1917	28/02/1917
War Diary	Belloy	01/03/1917	31/03/1917
Heading	5th Bn Durham L. Infantry Volume 24 March 1917		
War Diary	Pierregot	01/04/1917	02/04/1917
War Diary	Talmas	03/04/1917	03/04/1917
War Diary	Gezaincourt	04/04/1917	04/04/1917
War Diary	Bonnieres	05/04/1917	07/04/1917
War Diary	Berlencourt	08/04/1917	08/04/1917
War Diary	Liencourt	09/04/1917	10/04/1917
War Diary	Noyellette	11/04/1917	12/04/1917
War Diary	Arras	13/04/1917	26/04/1917
War Diary	Halloy	27/04/1917	30/04/1917
Heading	5 Bn Durham Light Infantry Volume 25 For Month Of April 1917		
War Diary	Halloy	01/05/1917	01/05/1917
War Diary	Coigneux	02/05/1917	02/05/1917
War Diary	Ficheux	03/05/1917	04/05/1917
War Diary	Coigneux	05/05/1917	05/05/1917
War Diary	Halloy	06/05/1917	17/05/1917
War Diary	Coigneux	18/05/1917	18/05/1917

War Diary	Douchy Les Ayette	19/05/1917	23/05/1917
War Diary	Coigneux	24/05/1917	31/05/1917
Heading	Volume 26 May 1917 5th Bn. Durham L. Infantry		
War Diary	Coigneux Chesnut Camp	01/06/1917	15/06/1917
War Diary	Boisleux	16/06/1917	17/06/1917
War Diary	La Trenches	18/06/1917	30/06/1917
War Diary	Boyelles	01/07/1917	03/07/1917
War Diary	Neuville Vittasse	04/07/1917	09/07/1917
War Diary	Trenches	10/07/1917	27/07/1917
War Diary	Neuville Vittasse	28/07/1917	04/08/1917
War Diary	Trenches	05/08/1917	20/08/1917
War Diary	Neuville Vittasse	21/08/1916	27/08/1916
War Diary	Bde Reserve	28/08/1917	31/08/1917
Heading	Volume 29 August 1917		
War Diary	Trenches	01/09/1917	01/09/1917
War Diary	Bde Reserve	05/09/1917	05/09/1917
War Diary	Trenches	09/09/1917	13/09/1917
War Diary	Northumberland Lines	13/09/1917	25/09/1917
War Diary	Trenches	25/09/1917	30/09/1917
War Diary	Neuville Vitasse	01/10/1917	03/10/1917
War Diary	Trenches	04/10/1917	06/10/1917
War Diary	Achiet-Le-Petit	07/10/1917	17/10/1917
War Diary	Rubrouck	18/10/1917	21/10/1917
War Diary	Ledringham	22/10/1917	22/10/1917
War Diary	Proven	23/10/1917	30/11/1917
War Diary	Nortleulingham	01/12/1917	02/12/1917
War Diary	Serques	03/10/1917	09/10/1917
War Diary	Brandhoek	10/12/1917	10/12/1917
War Diary	Trenches	11/12/1917	13/12/1917
War Diary	Potijze	16/12/1917	16/12/1917
War Diary	Brandhoek	17/12/1917	21/12/1917
War Diary	Potijze	22/12/1917	04/01/1918
War Diary	Winnezeele	05/01/1918	16/01/1918
War Diary	Quelmes	17/01/1918	28/01/1918
War Diary	Ypres	29/01/1918	31/01/1918
Heading	1/5 Durham L.I. Vol IX		
Heading	1/5 Durham L.I. Vol VII		

50TH DIVISION
150TH INFY BDE

5TH BN DURHAM LT INFY
1914 July ~~APR 1915~~-JAN 1918.

To 151 BDE . 50 DIV

50 DIV   BEF
150 BDE

5th Durham L. Inf

~~July 14 — July 15~~

1914 JLY — 1915 APL

2682

War Diary
5th Bn Durham
L Infty

29th July 1914
to
31st July 1915

APRIL 1915

50 DIVISION
150 Brigade

In France
Apl 1915

Hour-date & Station	Summary of events and Information	Remarks & Ref to App.
Deganwy July 29th 1914	Special Service Section (2 officers + 45 men) under Capt. Wilson & Lieut Hill - proceeded from Deganwy - concentrating at Stockton on Tees	
Stockton July 30th 1914	Special Service Section proceeded from Stockton to the War stations at South Gare and Hartlepool - Capt. Wilson @ South Gare with 20 men & Lieut Hill with 25 men at Hartlepool. <u>Duties</u> Protective duties on Batteries - guarding Government stores etc.	
Deganwy Aug. 3rd 1914	Annual Training @ Deganwy discontinued - Men proceeded to their respective Detachment Headquarters & were there disbanded	
Stockton Aug 4th 1914	Telegram ordering "Concentration" received at 10 am - Officers NCOs & men being ordered to concentrate at Headquarters Stockton-on-Tees. 5 pm - Telegram ordering "Mobilization" received - Mobilization notices posted - NCOs & Men	

Hour - date & Station	Summary of events and Information	Remarks & Ref to App.
August 4th 1914 Stockton	billeted in Drill Hall and Borough Hall - Officers at Trevelyan Hotel.	
Stockton August 5th 1914	B & C Coys under Capt Faber proceeded to South Gare @ 3.30pm - A.D.E.F.G.H. Coys to Hartlepool & West Hartlepool @ 4.0 oclock - being billeted as follows A Coy - Church Close Board Schools G & H Coys - Naval Barracks D.E & F Coys - Queens Rink	
August 6th to August 8th South Gare	B & C Coys at work making trenches for defence of South Gare from land attack - erecting wire entanglements etc - guarding batteries & position from surprise	
South Gare Aug 9th 1914	Orders to proceed to Newcastle into billets cancelled.	
South Gare Aug 10th 1914	Orders received to proceed to Hartlepool by boat - @ 12 noon - Arrived at Hartlepool @ 3 pm. being billeted as follows. B. Coy Church Close Schools C Coy Hart Road Schools	

Hour, date & Station	Summary of events and Information	Remarks, Ref to App.
West Hartlepool & Hartlepool August 6th to Aug 8th 1914	Companies engaged in making trenches & guarding coast - the allotted section being from Black Hut - N of Fever Hospital near Sectinctor to Old Pier - Hartlepool. Trenches also dug at Seaton Carew.	
August 9th to Sept 4th Hartlepool	All Companies engaged in a course of recruit training - part companies being detailed for protective duties on coast - batteries & Government Stores	
Hartlepool August 9th	The Battalion should have been relieved by the 3rd Batt Yorkshire Reg on this date and should have proceeded to Newcastle. This order cancelled.	
Aug. 14th	One officer (Lieut Pudan) and 50 men of F Coy proceeded to Castle Eden - billeting at "Parklands"	

Hour - date - Station	Summary of events and Information	Ref/App & Remarks
	Protective duties on roads railroads etc	
Hartlepool Aug 14th	E Coy under its own officers proceeded to Castle Eden in relief of F Coy	
Aug 16th to Sept 5th Hartlepool	Course of Recruit training done by all ranks - Musketry + Rifle exercises etc	
Hartlepool Sept 4th	Orders received to proceed to Hummerskmott Camp Darlington	
Sept 5th Hartlepool	The Battalion less E Coy entrained with 1st & 2nd line transport for Darlington in two trains at 3 o'clock pm.	
Sept 6th Darlington	Head quarters established at Hummerskmott Camp Darlington	
Darlington Sept 7th to 18th inclu.	Recruit training continued accompanied by two route marches per week	
Sept 18th Darlington	E Coy entrained at Castle Eden joined the Battalion at Hummerskmott.	

Hour, date & Station	Summary of Events and Information	Remarks Ref/App.
Sept 18th to Oct 5th Darlington	Course of Recruit training continued - accompanied by Route Marches & Miniature Range firing taking place at a bluff on the river. Range made by the Battalion	
Darlington Sept 9th to Sept 11th	All recruits who had not fired Table A - proceeded under Lt. Gloag to Measham Range & fired Table A.	
Darlington October 5th	Company training commenced. Programme made out by the Adjutant Capt. Hallcup & submitted to General Bush	
Darlington October 6th to " 15.	Company training proceeded with - Route Marches done twice weekly and one Company detailed for Miniature Range daily	
Oct 15th Darlington	Orders received to proceed Newcastle on 16th inst.	

Hour Date Station	Summary of events & Information	Remarks Ref App
Oct 16th Darlington	The Battalion entrained at Old New Castle Docks D'ton for Newcastle at 1 pm & detrained at Old New Castle Docks Forth Station Newcastle, proceeding to Billets in Canning Street Schools & Benwell Grange. Benwell - Officers less D. Coy & Head quarters - established at Benwell Grange.	
Oct 17th to " 24th Newcastle	Company training etc cont. Miniature range shooting taking place at a range situated at Charlotte Pit - Benwell Colliery	
October 25 Newcastle	Head quarters removed to Canning Street Schools & Officers, less D Coy officers & G H Coy officers who remained at Canning St Schools & Benwell Grange respectively, removed to West Oakwood Westgate Rd.	

Hour - Date & Station	Summary of Events & Information	Remarks & App Ref
Newcastle Oct 26th 15 Nov 2nd	Company training continued + miniature range practice etc	
Newcastle Nov 3rd	Alarm - order given from the York & Durham Brigade to "Stand by" in billets - all leave passes stopped by C.O. - Alarm caused by activity of German Fleet off Lowestoft	
Nov 5th	Order cancelled - Company training continued.	
Nov 5th Newcastle	37 Recruits (having fired Table A) came from Stockton to join Foreign Service Unit	
Nov 6th	Battalion paraded for Brigade & Divisional Manoeuvres at Cramlington - Fusiliers acting as defence & York & Durham Brigade with R.F.A. in attack	
Newcastle Nov 9th to Nov 12th	Battalion training commenced on Areas 5 & 7 (Newbiggin) & continued	

Hour, date & Station	Summary of Events & Information	Remarks & App Ref
Newcastle Nov. 13th	Alarm or order to "Stand by" in close proximity to billets received from Brigade at 6.30 pm. - All Officers & men recalled - no leave or passes issued. 111 Recruits (having fired Table A) came from Stockton to join Foreign Service Unit. 116 H.S. men returned to Stockton. Equipment taken from H.S. men to fit out F.S. men.	
Newcastle Nov 14th to Nov 15th	Battalion training continuing but order to "Stand by" in billets - still holding good.	
Newcastle Nov. 16th – 17th	Battalion Training continued as per programme on areas 5 & 2. (NEWBIGGIN).	

Hour, Date & Station	Summary of Events & Information	Remarks
Newcastle Nov. 18th	Battalion training continued. Draft of 3 Officers & 120 men N.C.O's of Reserve Battalion under Lieut. A.B Hill arrived from Stockton & proceeded to Westgate Rd. Schools. All Reserve men from Service Battalion join Reserve Battalion at Westgate Rd. Schools.	
Newcastle Nov. 19th – 20th	Battalion training continued & O.C. Coys arranged for Foreign Service Recruits to get miniature Range Practices.	
Newcastle Nov. 21st	Battalion ordered to parade on alarm Post at 6 A.M until further Orders.	
Newcastle Nov. 24th	Battalion training. 206 men of the Foreign Service Battalion arrive from Stockton Extract from "London Gazette" 13th Nov. 1914. Durham. L.I. Lieut. (Temp. Capt.) W.R.M. Hartcup to be Captain (Oct. 31. 1914)	
Nov. 25th	Recruits continue musketry at Ponteland from 25th to 28th under Lieut. Flogg.	

Hour, Date, Station	Summary of Events & Information	Remarks
Newcastle. Nov. 26th	Battalion training No. 3. area. Recruits continue musketry at Ponteland. Officers pay revised under Royal Warrant dated Nov. 24th 1914.	
Nov. 27th	Officers guards mounted at Forth Goods Station to guard ammunition. G.O.C in C again draws attention to the prevalence of cigarette smoking & directs it shall not be permitted while troops are under arms or on fatigues.	
Nov. 29th 30th	Battalion Parade, recruits under Capt. Raimes commence firing table "A" at Ponteland.	
Newcastle. Dec. 1.	Battalion training No. 4 area. Mrs. Pease of "Pendower House" places a Recreation Room & Bath at the disposal of the Battalion.	
Dec. 2nd	Battalion training — entrenching. Recruits under the Assistant Adjutant commence to fire Table A. at Ponteland. All units of Northumbrian Division T.F. ordered to consume reserve rations purchased on mobilization	

Hour, Date, Station	Summary of Events & Information	Remarks
Newcastle Dec. 3rd – Dec. 5th	Battalion training, recruits continued firing table "A" at Ponteland. Equipment of the whole Battalion checked. Capt. Walker, & 2/Lieuts. Crichton, Westoll, Robinson of the Reserve Battalion attached for Instruction.	
Dec. 9th	Battalion Parade, inspected in "Battalion in attack" by the G.O.C. in C. at Newbiggin. Bayonet Fighting continued in afternoons under Coy. arrangements	
Dec. 10th	Q.M. Sergt. T. Easley appointed Quartermaster to Reserve Battalion at Stockton & to hold rank of Hon. Lieut.	
Dec 11th	Battalion Training. Capt. Pindar, & 2/Lieuts Muirwood, Davis from the Reserve Battalion attached for training.	
Dec. 12th – 14th	Battalion Parade No. 2 area. Lecture to Coys. by Medical Officer on first aid. In view of fact that the Battalion will be firing its Musketry, O.C. Coys. gave all ranks Musketry Instruction in Barrack Room.	

Hour Date Station	Summary of Events & Information	Remarks
Newcastle Dec. 14th to 18th	Battalion Training Continued. Bayonet Fighting Instruction in afternoon. Troops still confined to Billets owing to scares on the N.E. Coast.	
Dec. 19th	Medical Officer continued Lectures on First Aid & Recruits recommended for Discharge as Medically Unfit were examined.	
Dec. 21st	Company Training to be carried out on No. 1 area. Capt. W.R.M. Hartcup placed on the sick list & Lieut. V.F. Gloag appointed acting Adjutant. A Regimental Recreation room was provided at the Co-operative Stores Elswick Rd. Newcastle.	
Dec. 21st — 26th	Battalion parades, Company training was continued. Standing to arms at 6 A.M. still continuing. All leave were cancelled for Christmas & troops had a Christmas Dinner followed by a dance in Billets.	

Hour, Date & Station	Summary of Events & Information	Remarks
Dec. 30th	Short route march in the morning followed in the afternoon by an Inter Coy. Cross Country race, over a course of about 6 miles.	
Newcastle. Dec. 31st	This was won by the old D Coy. Headquarters & A, C, D, F & G Coys. entrained at New Castle Dock, Forth Goods Station 10.15 AM & proceeded to Neasham to perform Musketry training. Headquarters at Hurworth Hall, Coys. Billets at Hurworth, Neasham, & Ropners Convalescent Home Dinsdale. E. & H Coys. remained behind at Canning St. Newcastle under the command of Major H. Ensor & continued carrying out Company Training.	
Hurworth. Jan. 1st 1915	Musketry parade 8.15 AM. & firing carried out from 9.30 – 12.30 P.M. 1.0 – 3.30 P.M. Tea ration was served on the range. Half Coys. not firing carried out Route marches & instruction in Musketry.	

Hour, date & Station	Summary of Events & Information	Remarks
Hurworth. Jan. 2nd — Jan. 11th 1915	Musketry Instruction & Firing being continued at Hurworth. E & H Coys. leave Newcastle & move to Hurworth. A, D & G Coys. entrain at New Cattle Dock Darlington & return to Newcastle.	
Jan. 12th — 22nd.	E & H Coys, casuals & recruits continued firing their Musketry Courses between these dates.	
Jan. 22nd.	The Battalion entrained at New Cattle Dock Darlington & returned to Newcastle. All fbtblk lines inspected by the C.O. during the course of the morning.	
Newcastle. Jan. 23d	On returning to Newcastle the four Company organization was adopted as below. Present A & B. new title A Capt. Raimes " C & G. " " B. Major. Ensor. " D & E " " C. Capt. Pearson " F & H " " D. Capt. Faber	

HOUR. DATE. STATION	SUMMARY OF EVENTS & INFORMATION	REMARKS
Newcastle. Jan. 27th	Battalion paraded on alarm post at 6 A.M. Company training continued. At night the Battalion practised entrenching by night.	
Newcastle. Feb. 1.	Company training continued. Battalion entrenching by night.	
Feb. 2.	Lieut Littleboy & 2 Lieuts Laycock, Jones & Hollings of reserve Battalion attached for instruction.	
Feb. 3.	Bayonet instruction commenced by C. Sergt. Buchan with platoons. Officers & N.C.O's attended a lecture by Dr. Willie Maguire at the Empire on "Modern scientific innovations in the war". Capt. W.R.M. Hartcup appointed Brigade Major to York & Durham Brigade (Reserve) Battalion to be known in future as 1/5th Durham. L.I.	
Feb. 8th	Lieut Kitching & Bagley, Vane-Tempest attached for instruction.	

Hour. Date. Station	Summary of Events & Information	Remarks
Newcastle. Feb 9th	The 1st line York & Durham Brigade under Lt. Col. G. O Spence provided for a route march & manoeuvres. This Battalion acted as an advance guard under Major B.G.D. Bigge.	
Feb. 10th	Brigade Parade. "Brigade in attack" 5th Durham Light Infy. was under the command of Major Bigge.	
Feb. 12th	Battalion Parade, firing on the miniature Ranges at Benwell Colliery & Benwell House Hotel was continued from this date.	
Feb. 13th	All men not yet fired Recruits course paraded for special instruction in Musketry. Lieut Raimer & II Lieut F Tournend attached for instruction. Sanitary Squads & Water duty men lectured to by Medical Officer.	
Feb. 15th	Brigade Route march, the Battalion formed main body & rear guard. Brigade Duties resumed by this Battalion.	

Hour, Date, Station	Summary of Events & Information	Remarks
Newcastle Feb. 17th	Battalion paraded for Brigade manoeuvres, and rendezvoused at Kenton Cross Roads for the purpose of carrying out an attack on an entrenched position.	
Feb 18th	Officers & N.C.O's attended an instructional Lecture at Lit. & Phil. Hall Newcastle by Dr Ker on Hygiene.	
Feb. 19th	Recruits & Casuals proceeded by road to Ponteland under Lieut. Moscrop to fire Musketry Course.	
Feb. 22nd	Brigade Route March. 5th Durham. L.I. formed main body.	
Feb. 23d	Officers & NCO's attended a lecture by Capt. Macqueen R.E. on "Cooperation of Field Engineers with other Arms."	
Feb. 25th	Lecture to Officers & N.C.O's by Capt. Douglas R.E. on Miscellaneous Field Engineering	
Feb. 27th	Battalion practised entrenching by night.	

Hour Date Station	Summary of Events & Information	Remarks
Newcastle. March 1.	Brigade Route March & Manoeuvre. 5th Durham L.I. forms main Body. Rendezvous old race course.	
March 3rd	Brigade attack. 1st line 5th Durham L.I. represents the enemy & holds an entrenched position at High Callerton.	
March 4th	Musketry Casuals under Lieut Moscrop proceed to Ponteland to fire Musketry Course. Extract London Gazette 4/3/15. Lieut Gloag to be Captain & Adjutant vice Capt. Hartcup.	
March 8th	Brigade Concentration scheme & Billeting at Killingworth. Inspected by Divisional Staff.	
March 9th	Musketry Party returned from Ponteland. Lecture to Officers & N.C.O's by Major Thomson Artillery on "Cooperation of Artillery with other Arms." A & B Coys. change Billets to Westgate Rd. School. Transport & Machine Guns to Benwell Grange.	

Hour Date Station	Summary of Events & Information	Remarks
Hurworth March 10th	Brigade carried out an attack on an enemy in an entrenched position near Black Colliston. 5th Durham L.I. & 1 Battery R.F.A. represented enemy.	
March 13th	A Coy under Capt: Raimes proceeded to Ponteland to fire Field Practices. Remainder, Battalion training and night operations.	
March 15th	B Coy under Major Enros proceeded to Ponteland to fire Field Practices. Remainder carried out Billeting Schemes at Whickham & Brigade concentration.	
March 16th	C Coy under Capt. Pearson fired Field Practices at Ponteland.	
March 17th	D Coy fired Field Practices. Remainder assembled at Ludwick for acting as enemy for the Brigade to practise a retirement. Cancelled owing to snow storm.	
March 18th	Draft of 16 men & Lieut Williams join the Battalion from the reserve.	

Hour Date Station	Summary of Events & Information	Remarks
Newcastle March. 22nd	Brigade inspected on Town Moor by the G.O.C. in C. In the morning a Kit inspection was held by the C.O. Lecture in evening by Dr Cornish on the "Strategical Geography of the War"	
March 23d	Officers commence signalling class under Sergt. Walker.	
March. 24th	Casuals proceed under Lieut Marsh to Ponteland for field Practice. Battalion took part in Divisional Operations.	
March. 26th	A & B Coys were inspected by the C.O. Equipment & kits. Remainder carry out Company Training under Major. B.G.D. Biggs.	
March. 27th	Kit inspection by C.O of C & D Coys.	
March. 29th	Battalion took part in a Brigade Outpost Scheme line Pt. 344 to Fallows.	

Hour Date Station	Summary of events & information	Remarks

Nevinstall.

April 1st — Company Training continued. Medical Inspection of complete Battalion.

April 3rd — Company Training. Medical Inspection of Casuals; Inter Platoon Cross Country race won by No. 9 C Coy. Last week.

April 5th — Running Drill & Bolt drill before breakfast. Company Training Continued.

April 8th — Casuals (23) proceeded to Portland under Lieut. Marsh to join Mess Relay. 75 Recruits were included in this month. Officers & Mess Room cancelled preparatory to moving abroad.

April 12–13 — Company Officers had busy days for Company Training & final preparations for going abroad, issues of Kit etc. were made.

April 14th — Parade under Company arrangements, fitting out all kit. Transport & Machine gun personnel entrained at OLS Cattle Docks, Leith Goods Station for Southampton at 2.30 a.m. under Capt. H. Watson, & Lieuts. Edson & Hesslin Jun.

1/5th DURHAM. L.I.

Sheets from 1 to 21

Hour-date & Station	Summary of events and Information	Remarks & Refs. app.
Deganwy July 29th 1914	Special Service Section (2 Officers + 45 men) under Capt. Wilson & Lieut Hill - proceeded from Deganwy - concentrating at Stockton on Tees	Duplicate
Stockton July 30th 1914	Special Service Section proceeded from Stockton to the War Stations at South Gare and Hartlepool - Capt. Wilson @ South Gare with 20 men & Lieut Hill with 25 men at Hartlepool. Duties Protective duties on Batteries - guarding Government stores etc.	
Deganwy Aug. 3rd 1914	Annual Training @ Deganwy discontinued - Men proceeded to their respective detachment Head quarters & were there disbanded	
Stockton Aug 4th 1914	Telegram ordering "Concentration" received at 10 am. Officers N.C.O's & men being ordered to concentrate at Head quarters Stockton-on-Tees. 5 pm. - Telegram ordering "Mobilization" received - Mobilization Notices posted - N.C.O's & Men	

Hour, date & Station	Summary of events and Information	Remarks & Ref to App
August 4th 1914 Stockton	billet'ed in Bull Hall and Borough Hall - Officers at Trevelyan Hotel.	
Stockton August 5th 1914	B & C Coys under Capt Faber proceeded to South Gare @ 3:30 pm - A. D. E. F. G. H Coys to Hartlepool & West Hartlepool @ 4.0 o'clock - being billeted as follows A Coy - Church Close Board Schools G & H Coys - Naval Barracks D. E. & F Coys - Queens Rink	
August 6th to August 8th South Gare	B & C Coys at work making trenches for defence of South Gare from land attack - erecting wire entanglements etc - guarding batteries & position from surprise	
South Gare Aug 9th 1914	Orders to proceed to Newcastle into billets cancelled.	
South Gare Aug 10th 1914	Orders received to proceed to Hartlepool by boat @ 12 noon. Arrived at Hartlepool @ 3 pm. being billet'ed as follows. B. Coy Church Close Schools C Coy Hart Road Schools	

Hour, date & Station	Summary of events and Information	Remarks, Ref to App.
West Hartlepool & Hartlepool August 6th to Aug 8th 1914	Companies engaged in making trenches & guarding Coast - the allotted section being from Black Hut - N of Fever Hospital near Destructor to Old Pier - Hartlepool. Trenches also dug at Seaton Carew.	
August 9th to Sept 4th Hartlepool	All Companies engaged in a course of recruit training - part companies being detailed for protective duties on Coast - batteries & Government Stores.	
Hartlepool August 9th	The Battalion should have been relieved by the 3rd Batt. Yorkshire Reg on this date and ~~then~~ should have proceeded to Newcastle. This order cancelled.	
Aug. 14th	One officer (Lieut Pudan) and 50 men of F Coy proceeded to Castle Eden - billeting at "Parklands"	

Hour - date + Station	Summary of events and Information	Ref App. + Remarks
	Protective duties on roads railroads etc.	
Hartlepool Aug 14th	E Coy under its own officers proceeded to Castle Eden in relief of F Coy	
Aug 16th to Sept 5th Hartlepool	Course of Recruit training done by all ranks - Musketry + Rifle exercises etc	
Hartlepool Sept 4th	Orders received to proceed to Hummersknot Camp Darlington	
Sept 5th Hartlepool	The Battalion less E Coy entrained with 1st & 2nd line transport for Darlington in two trains at 3 o'clock pm.	
Sept 6th Darlington	Headquarters established at Hummersknot Camp Darlington.	
Darlington Sept 7th to 18th incl.	Recruit training continued accompanied by two route marches per week	
Sept 18th Darlington	E Coy entrained at Castle Eden + joined the Battalion at Hummersknot.	

Hour, date & Station	Summary of Events and Information	Remarks R/App
Sept 18th to Oct 5th Darlington	Course of Recruit training is continued - accompanied by Route Marches & Miniature Range firing, taking place at a bluff on the river. Range made by the Battalion	
Darlington Sept 9th to Sept 11th	All recruits who had not fired Table A. proceeded under Lt. Gloag to Needham Range & fired Table A.	
Darlington October 5th	Company training commenced Programme made out by the Adjutant Capt. Hartcup & submitted to General Bush	
Darlington October 5th to " 15.	Company training proceeded with - Route Marches done twice weekly and one Company detailed for Miniature Range daily	
Oct 15th Darlington	Orders received to proceed to Newcastle on 16th inst.	

Hour date Station	Summary of events & Information	Remarks & Ref App
Oct 16th Darlington	The Battalion entrained at Old New Castle docks S/tn for Newcastle at 1 pm & detrained at Old & New Castle docks. for the Station Newcastle - proceeding to Billets in Canning Street Schools & Benwell Grange. Benwell - Officers less D. Coy & Head quarters - established at Benwell Grange.	
Oct 17th to " 24th Newcastle	Company training etc cont. Miniature range shooting taking place at a range situated at Charlotte pit - Benwell Colliery	
October 25th Newcastle	Headquarters removed to Canning Street Schools & Officers, less D Coy Officers & C/H Coy Officers who remained at Canning St. Schools & Benwell Grange respectively removed to West Oakwood Westgate Rd.	

Hour - date & Station	Summary of Events & Information	Remarks & App Ref
Newcastle. Oct 26th to Nov. 2nd	Company training continued + miniature range practice etc.	
Newcastle. Nov. 3rd	Alarm - order given from the York & Durham Brigade to "Stand by" in billets - all leave & passes stopped by C.O. - Alarm caused by activity of German Fleet off Lowestoft	
Nov 5th	Order cancelled - Company training continued.	
Nov 6th Newcastle	37 Recruits (having fired Table A) came from Stockton to join Foreign Service Unit	
Nov 6th	Battalion paraded for Brigade & Divisional Manœuvres at Cramlington - Fusiliers acting as defence North & Durham Brigade with R.F.A. in attack.	
Newcastle Nov. 9th to Nov 12th	Battalion training commenced on Areas 6 & 4 (Newbiggin) & continued.	

Hour date & Station	Summary of Events & Information	Remarks & App Ref
Newcastle Nov. 13th	A damn or order to "Stand by" in close proximity to billets received from Brigade at 6.30 p.m. - all Officers & men recalled & no leave or passes issued. 111 Recruits (having fired Table A) came from Stockton to join Foreign Service Unit & 115 H.S. men returned to Stockton. Equipment taken from H.S. men to fit out F.S. men.	
Newcastle Nov 14th to Nov 15th	Battalion Training continued but order to "Stand by" for billets - still holding good.	
Newcastle Nov. 16th – 17th	Battalion Training continued as per programme on cards 5.2.B. (Newbiggin).	

Hour, Date & Station.	Summary of Events & Information	Remarks.
Newcastle. Nov. 18th	Battalion training continued. Draft of 3 Officers & 120 men N.C.O's of Reserve Battalion under Lieut. A.B Hill arrived from Stockton & proceeded to Westgate Rd. Schools. All Reserve men from Service Battalion join Reserve Battalion at Westgate Rd. Schools.	
Newcastle Nov. 19th - 20th	Battalion training continued & O.C Coys arranged for Foreign Service Recruits to get Miniature Range Practice.	
Newcastle. Nov. 21st	Battalion ordered to parade on alarm Post at 6 A.M until further Orders.	
Newcastle. Nov. 24th	Battalion training. 206 men of the Foreign Service Battalion arrive from Stockton Extract from "London Gazette" 13th Nov. 1914. Durham. L.I. Lieut. (Temp. Capt.) W.R.M Hankey to be Captain (Oct. 31. 1914)	
Nov. 25th	Recruits continue musketry at Ponteland Nov. 25th to 28th under Lieut. Gloag.	

Hour. Date Station	Summary of Events & Information	Remarks
Newcastle. Nov. 26th	Battalion training No. 3 area. Recruits continue musketry at Ponteland. Officers pay revised under Royal Warrant dated Nov. 24th 1914.	
Nov. 27th	Officers guards mounted at Forth Goods Station to guard ammunition. G.O.C in C again draws attention to the prevalence of cigarette smoking & directs it shall not be permitted while troops are under arms or on fatigues.	
Nov. 29th & 30th	Battalion Parade, recruits under Capt. Raimes commence firing Table "A" at Ponteland	
Newcastle. Dec. 1.	Battalion training No. 4 area. Mrs. Pease of "Pendower House" places a Recreation Room & Bath at the disposal of the Battalion.	
Dec. 2nd	Battalion training — entrenching. Recruits under the Assistant Adjutant commence to fire Table A. at Ponteland. All units of Northumbrian Division T.F. ordered to consume reserve rations purchased on mobilization	

Hour, Date Station	Summary of Events & Information	Remarks
Newcastle Dec. 3d – Dec. 5th	Battalion Training, recruits continue firing table "A" at Ponteland. Equipment of the whole Battalion checked. Capt. Walker, & 2nd Lieuts. Wrightson, Birtall, Robinson of the Reserve Battalion attached for Instruction.	
Dec. 9th	Battalion Parade, was judged in "Battalion in attack" by the G.O.C. in C. at Newbiggin. Bayonet Fighting continued in afternoon under Coy. arrangements.	
Dec. 10th	Q.M. Sergt. T. Casley appointed Quartermaster to Reserve Battalion at Stockton & to hold rank of Hon. Lieut.	
Dec. 11th	Battalion Training. Capt. Pindar, & 2nd Lieuts. Jack Wood, Davies from the Reserve Battalion attached for training.	
Dec. 12th – 14th	Battalion Parade No. 2 dress. Lectures to Coys by Medical Officer on first aid. In view of fact that the Battalion will be firing its musketry, O.C. Coys. gave all ranks musketry Instruction in Barrack Room.	

Hour Date Station	Summary of Events & Information	Remarks
Newcastle. Dec. 14th to 18th	Battalion Training continued. Bayonet Fighting instruction in afternoons. Troops still confined to Billets owing to scares on the N.E. coast.	
Dec. 19th	Medical Officer continued Lectures on First Aid & Recruits recommended for Discharge as Medically Unfit were examined.	
Dec. 21st	Company Training to be carried out on No. 1 area. Capt. W.R.M. Hartcup placed on the sick list & Lieut. V.F. Glagg appointed acting Adjutant. A Regimental Recreation room was provided at the Co-operative Stores Church Rd. Newcastle.	
Dec. 21st — 26th — 144th	Battalion parades, Company training was continued. Standing to arms at 6 A.M. still continuing. All leaves were cancelled for Christmas & troops had a Christmas Dinner followed by a dance in Billets.	

Hour, Date & Station	Summary of Events & Information	Remarks
Dec. 30th	Short route march in the morning followed in the afternoon by an Inter Coy. cross country race, over a course of about 6 miles. This was won by the old D Coy.	
Newcastle. Dec. 31st	Headquarters & A, C, D, F & G Coys. entrained at New Castle Dock Forth Goods Station 10:15 AM & proceeded to Hexham to perform Musketry training. Headquarters at Hexham Hall, Coys. billeted at Hexham, Wear ham, & Rothmans Convalescent Home, Dinsdale. E. & H Coys. remained behind at Canning St. Newcastle under the command of Major H. Cookson, & continued carrying out Company Training.	
Hexham. Jan. 1st 1915	Musketry parade 8.15 AM. & firing carried out from 9.30 – 12.30 P.M. 1.0 – 3.30 P.M. Tea ration was served on the range. Half Coys. not firing carried out Route marches & instruction in Musketry.	

Hour, date & Station	Summary of Events & Information	Remarks
Hurworth. Jan. 2nd – Jan. 11th 1915.	Musketry Instruction & Firing being continued at Hurworth. E & H Coys. leave Newcastle & move to Hurworth. A. D & G. Coys. entrain at Newcastle Dock Darlington & return to Newcastle.	
Jan. 12th – 22nd.	E & H Coys, cadres & recruits continued firing their Musketry Courses between these dates.	
Jan. 22nd.	The Battalion entrained at New Castle Dock Darlington & returned to Newcastle. All ranks were inspected by the C.O. during the course of the morning.	
Newcastle Jan. 23rd	On returning to Newcastle the four Company organization was adopted as below. Present A & B. new title A. Capt. Raimes " C & G " " B. Major Enson. " D & E " " C. Capt. Pearson " F & H " " D. Capt. Faber	

HOUR. DATE. STATION	SUMMARY OF EVENTS & INFORMATION	REMARKS.

Newcastle.
Jan. 27th

Battalion paraded on alarm post at 6 A.M. Company training continued. At night the Battalion practised entrenching by night.

Newcastle.
Feb. 1.

Company training continued. Battalion entrenched by night.

Feb. 2.

Lieut Lithgoe & 2 Lieuts Laycock, Jones & Williams of reserve Battalion attached for instruction.

Feb. 3.

Bayonet instruction commenced by C. Sergt. Buchan with platoons.

Newcastle.

Officers & N.C.O's attended a lecture by Dr. Mille Maguire at the Empire on "Modern scientific innovations in the War".

Capt. W.R.M. Hartcup appointed Brigade Major to York & Durham Brigade (Reserve)

Battalion to be known in future as 1/5th Durham L.I.

Feb. 8th

Lieut Kitching & Bagley, Vane-Tempest attached for instruction.

HOUR. DATE. STATION	SUMMARY OF EVENTS & INFORMATION	REMARKS
Newcastle Feb. 9th	The 1st Line York & Durham Brigade under Lt. Col. J. O Spence paraded for a route march & manœuvres. This Battalion acted as an advance guard under Major B.G.D. Biggs.	
Feb. 10th	Brigade Parade. "Brigade in attack" 5th Durham Light Infy. were under the command of Major Biggs.	
Feb. 12th	Battalion Parade, firing on the Miniature Range at Benwell Colliery & Benwell House Hotel was continued from this date.	
Feb. 13th	All men not yet fired Recruits Courses paraded for special instruction in musketry. Lieut Rowan & II Lieut F Townsend attached for instruction Sanitary Squad & water duty men lectured to by Medical Officer.	
Feb. 15th	Brigade Route march the Battalion formed main body & rear guard. Brigade Duties assumed by this Battalion	

Hour, Date, Station	Summary of Events & Information	Remarks
Newcastle. Feb. 17th	Battalion paraded for Brigade manoeuvres, and render-vouzed at Kenton Bar Roads for the purpose of carrying out an attack on an entrenched position.	
Feb. 18th	Officers & N.C.O's attended an instructional lecture at Lt. Phil Hall Newcastle by Dr. Kerr on Hygiene.	
Feb. 19th	Recruits & Cor.[?] proceeded by road to P.[?]land under Lieut. [?] to [?] Musketry Course.	
Feb. 22nd	Brigade Route March. 5th Durham L.I. formed main body.	
Feb. 23d	Officers & N.C.O's attended a lecture by Capt. McQueen R.E. on Cooperation of Field Engineers with other Arms.	
Feb. 25th	Lecture to Officers & N.C.O's by Capt. Douglas R.E. on [?] Elementary Field Engineering	
Feb. 27th	Battalion practised entrenching by night.	

Hour Date Station	Summary of Events & Information	Remarks
Newcastle. March 1.	Brigade Route March & Manoeuvres. 5th Durham L.I. forms main Body. Rendezvous old race course.	
March 3d	Brigade attack. 1st line 5th Durham L.I. represents the enemy & holds an entrenched position at High Callerton.	
March 4th	Musketry Cadets under Lieut Moncrieff proceed to Portland to fire Musketry Courses. Extract London Gazette. 4/3/15. Lieut Glossop to be Captain & Adjutant vice Capt. Hartcup.	
March 8th	Brigade Concentration & review & B Blehes at Killingworth Inspected by Divisional Staff.	
March 9th	Musketry Party returned from Pontland. Lecture to Officers & NCO's by Major Thomson Artillery on "Co-ordination of Artillery with other Arms." A & B Coys change Billets to Westgate Rd Schools. Transport & Machine Guns to Benwell Grange.	

Hour Date Station	Summary of Events & Information	Remarks
Wareham March 12th	Brigade carried out an attack on an enemy in an entrenched position near Black Hilston. 1st Durham L.I. & 1 Battery R.F.A. represented enemy.	
March 13th	A Coy under Capt. Raven proceeded to Portland to fire Field Practices. Remainder Battalion training and night operations.	
March 15th	B Coy under Major Evans proceeded to Portland to fire Field Practices. Remainder carried out Billeting Scheme at Chickham & Brigade Concentration.	
March 16th	C Coy under Capt. Pearson fired Field Practices at Portland.	
March 17th	D Coy fired Field Practices. Remainder assembled at Rideout for acting as enemy for the Brigade to practice a retirement. Cancelled owing to snow storm.	
March 18th	Draft of 16 men & Lieut Wilson join the Battalion from the Reserve.	

Hour Date Station	Summary of Events & Information	Remarks
Newcastle March 22nd	Brigade inspected on Town Moor by the G.O.C. in C. In the morning a Kit inspection was held by the C.O. Lecture in evening by Dr Cornish on the "Strategical geography of the war"	
March 23rd	Officers commenced signalling class under Sergt Walker	
March 24th	Carriers proceeded under Lieut March to Ponteland & had field practices. Battalion took part in Divisional Operations.	
March 26th	A & B Coys kits inspected by the C.O. Equipment & kits Remainder carry out Company Training under Major B.G.D. Biggs.	
March 27th	Kit inspection by C.O of C & D Coys.	
March 29th	Battalion took part in a Brigade Outpost Scheme line Pt. 3+4 to Felthouse.	

150th Inf.Bde.
50th Div.

Battn. disembarked
Boulogne from
England 17.4.15.

WAR DIARY

1/5th BATTN. THE DURHAM LIGHT INFANTRY.

A P R I L

1 9 1 5

1/5th Battalion The Durham Light Infantry.

April 1915

	1/5 D.L.I.	21
Hour Date Station	Summary of events & information	Remarks
Newcastle April 1	Company Training continued, Medical Inspection of complete Battalion.	
April 3rd	Company Training, Medical Inspection of Casuals, Inter Platoon Cross Country race won by No 2. C Coy. Lieut. Meik.	
April 5th	Running Drill & Bolt drill before breakfast. Company Training Continued.	
April 8th	Casuals (23) proceed to Portland under Lieut Marwood to fire Musketry Course. 75 Recruits were included in this number. Officers & Mens leave cancelled preparatory to moving abroad.	
April 12-14	Company Officers had their Coys for Company Training & final preparations for going abroad, issues of Kit etc. were made.	
April 14th	Parades under Company arrangements — fitting out with Kit. Transport & Machine gun personnel entrained at Old Cattle Dock Forth Goods Station for Southampton at 12.30 A.M, under Capt. H. Wilson, & Lieuts. Robson & Hessler Sum.	

1/5 D — 1   22

Hour Date Station	Summary of events – information	Remarks
April 15th	Battalion was inspected in the morning at Stalyford by Rowland Burdon Hon. Colonel of the 5th D.whams L.I.	
April 16th	The Battalion entrained in two halves at Central Station Newcastle and left at 1.30 P.M. en route for Folkestone arriving at 1 AM the next day. Reserve Battalion paraded	
April 17th Boulogne	Landed at Boulogne after a very good crossing and after disembarking climbed up the long hill out of the town up to ST. Martin's Camp where we were under Canvas until the evening. In the evening we marched to Pont-du-Briques where we entrained for Cassel.	
April 18th	We detrained at Cassel & marched out to Steinvoorde where we Billeted in outlying farm Houses.	
April 19th Steinvoorde	Paraded under Coy. arrangements	

Hour date Station	Summary of events and information	Remarks
April 20th	Coy. Trainings. Officers were held out at night in assembling at alarm posts.	
April 21st	Battalion practised as test concentration on Battalion alarm post.	
April 22nd	Battalion inspected in the morning by General Sir W. Lindsay K.C.B. D.S.O	
April 23d	Alarm given early in the morning for a move and left about mid-day in motor buses, went into a rest camp for a few hours, rest camp near NOORDHOF.	
April 24th	Left the rest camp at 1 AM & moved towards the YSER canal & halted in a field for some hours. About midday the Battalion crossed the canal under shrapnel fire & moved into support trenches near ST. JEAN, where we suffered several casualties from shrapnel fire, Lieut. E. W. Fahes being severely wounded.	
April 25th 3 AM	Moved out along the ST. JEAN FORTUIN road & took up a line of trenches behind FORTUIN.	

Hour date Station	Summary of Events & Information	Remarks
	from which we moved back to the Verlorenhoek road. After a short rest we advanced to the attack on the FORTUIN position & took up a line of trenches north of the ST. Jean — ST. JULIEN Rd. Here suffered several casualties Lieut. J. C. Brown being wounded.	
April 26th ST. Julien.	This day was spent in these trenches which were under heavy shell fire the whole time, the Battalion had got split up after the attack & remnants of companies trickled in.	
April 27th	Moved from these trenches & took up a position in the first line trenches having the 5TH. YORKS on our right & the ROYAL IRISH on our left.	
April 28th	Continued to hold this position under shell fire this being several casualties. We were relieved at 11 P.M by the 4TH. E. YORKS. & returned to rest camp B near BRIERLEN.	

Hour, date & station	Summary of Events & occurrences	Remarks
Rest Camp near BRIERLEN April 29th	Owing to Rest Camps being under danger of fire from shells, all men turned out to entrench before breakfast. Rested during the day. Prepared for a move at 7 P.M but it was cancelled & the night was spent in camp.	
April 30th BRIERLEN.	Casualties to date. Officers Killed nil. " wounded. 3. Capt. Glossop. 28 April Lieut E. Fahns. 24th. Lieut J.C. Brown. 24th. Men. killed. 33. " wounded. 93. " missing. 25.	

150th Inf.Bde.
50th Div.

1/5th BATTN. THE DURHAM LIGHT INFANTRY.

M A Y

1 9 1 5

1/5th Battalion The Durham Light Infantry.

May 1915

Date	
May 1st	Spent the day in camp & moved at 8 P.M in the direction of POPPERINGHE went by a cross country route to avoid shell fire & the village of VLAMERTINGHE. Bivouacked in an open field about 3 miles from POPPERINGHE & owing to danger of shell fire proceeded to dig in.
2nd May. Near POPPERINGHE	Spent day in the field here, & were not shelled though several hostile aeroplanes passed over. At 8.30 P.M left for Steinvoorde where we billeted for the night. The march was very long & trying & many fell out.
3d May. STEINVOORDE	Stood by here until 5.30 P.M & then moved into billets about two miles from Steinvoorde, named ST. LAURENT, where we billeted in farm houses.
4th May ST. LAURENT	In Billets at St. Laurent addressed in the morning by Field Marshall Sir John French.
5th May.	In Billets parades under Coy. arrangements
6th May.	At Billets parades as before.
7th May	At Billets parades as before, several platoons enabled to Bath in Steinvoorde. Message received from Brigade saying that this unit formed part of the general Army Reserve under direct orders of General H.Q's. Troops advised to be ready to move at an hours notice.
May 8th	Standing by.

Hour date Station	Summary of events & information	Remarks
May 9th ST. Laurent	Church Parade, Battalion concentrated at 2.15 PM & moved by Motor Buss up to bivouac outside Poperinghe on S side of Ypres–Poperinghe Rd.	
May 10th	At Concentration camp.	
May 11th	York & Durham Brigade left at 2 P.M for camp near Vlamertinge dug in on arrival.	
May 12th Hooge.	Battalion less H.Q's moved into trenches through Ypres. in Sanctuary & Hooge woods. Companies split up & attached to various Regiments, Royal Scots, 5th Hussars, 16th Lancers.	
May 13th & 14th	Companies moved about in turn from firing line to supports & reserve trenches.	
May 14th – 22nd	Companies attached to 2nd Cavalry Brigade & carrying on as before. Chiefly in support to Hussars & Lancers.	
May 23rd	Germans attacked our trench on N.E side of Sanctuary wood. Some Companies gassed & many casualties.	
May 25th	Battalion less C Company relieved & returned to C rest camp near Brielen. C hung on to switch trench.	
May 26th	C Cy. & stragglers return to rest camp.	

Hour Date Place	Summary of events & information	Remarks
May 26th C rest camp	Battalion concentrated & resting. Digging parties sent out to dig on G.H.Q. line at Ypres. Casualties Dating from April 30th. Died of wounds received on the 24th. J.C.D. Brown. Officers Killed. Capt. R.W. Pearson. Wounded. Lieut. G.L. Rutherford. Capt. H.G. Faber. Capt. J. Blumer. Lieut. G. Ashworth. Lieut. J. D. Brown. Gassed. Lieut. J.K. Hessler. Lieut. N. Saddler. 2nd Lieut. Walker came from Reserve on the 20th & returned sick on the following day.	
May 27th C Camp	Battalion remained at & rest camp this day. sent out a digging party to make communication trenches between G.H.Q lines near Lake &Z oonebeke	
28th	Battalion left C camp at 6 P.M. & marched to B rest camp South of Vlamertinghe which had been vacated by 1st Cavalry Division.	
May 29th B rest camp Vlamertinghe	From May 29th to June 4th the Battalion remained here under half hour notice.	

Hour Date lation	Summary of events & Information	Remarks

Messages Received.

To. 4th Yorks & 5th D.L.I. 29th May.

150. Bde. less two Battalions will be in reserve to General Kavanagh's Force. Units will be held in readiness to move to concentration point at half an hour's notice from receipt of orders at their billets. Points of concentration for Bde is on VLAMERTINGHE — VORMEZEELE road heads at T roads. H.16A 4th Yorks then 5th D.L.I.

From. 150th Inf. Bde.

8.0. A.M.

150th Inf.Bde.
50th Div.

1/5th BATTN. THE DURHAM LIGHT INFANTRY.

J U N E

1 9 1 5

1/5th Battalion The Durham Light Infantry.

June 1915

June 4th
6 P.M.
B camp
Vlamertinghe.
Battalion moved to Bivouacs in open field on VLAMMERTINGHE - OUDERDOM road. Ordered to move to trenches on the evening of the 5th but order was cancelled until following day.

June 6th
6 P.M.
Battalion moved to trenches 1 to 6 between HOOGE & HILL 60, went via KRUISSTRAAT & LAKE ZILLEBECKE.
1 & 2 trenches.   C Coy.
3 & 4   A Coy.
5 & 6.   B + D Coy.

Hour. Date Station	Summary of Events & Information.	Remarks
June 9th to June 23d	In trenches 5 & 6. SANCTUARY-WOOD. Two companies occupying trenches & supports two companies being held in reserve in SANCTUARY-WOOD.	
June 23d 1 A.M.	Battalion relieved by Sherwood Foresters (N. MIDLAND DIVIS.) and returned to F Camp VLAMMERTINGHE.	
24th	At F Camp. Casualties dating from May 25th to June. 23d.	
DETTINGEN HUTS.	Officers. NIL. Men. 10 killed. 25 wounded.	
June 25th 8.15 AM	Battalion left F Camp & moved into Dettingen huts in new area S. 5 B. LOCRE - DRANACOURT.	
26th	In huts, day spent with Bathing Parades, fitting of equipment & Parades under Coy. arrangements.	
27th	Church Parade at 9.30 A.M. in camp.	
28th	Running Drill in morning. Coy. Officers went up to view new trenches. 6.30 P.M. Battalion moved to take over new trenches in front of MESSINES. distribution as follows. H.Q's at R.E. FARM. in support. A. Coy. " " " in support.	

Date Time Place	Summary of events & information	Remarks
June 28th	B. Coy. less 2 platoons in D. 14 trench. C Coy + 2 platoons of B in D. 4 trench. D Coy in D. 3 trench.	
June 29th " 30th	Battalion occupying trenches in trenches.	

150th Inf.Bde.
50th Div.

1/5th BATTN. THE DURHAM LIGHT INFANTRY.

J U L Y

1 9 1 5

1/5th Battalion The Durham Light Infantry.

July 1915

July 1st — Battalion inspected in trenches by General the Earl of Cavan in command of the Northumbrian Division T.F.

July 2nd — Battalion relieved by the 5th Yorks. Regiment at 10.30.P.M & returned to DETTINGEN HUTS, DRANACOURT. DRANOUTRE.

July 3d — In huts, Battalion Bathing parade & Coy. inspections.

July 4th — Church Parade at 9.30.A.M followed by Commanding Officers inspection. Casualties from 28th to July 2nd 2 men killed one wounded. Reinforcement of 75 men arrived from England under Capt. Wilkin

July 5th — Early morning Parade & Route March under Coy. arrangements. Battalion inspected by Major General Sir Charles Ferguson

July 6th — Early morning parade & usual inspections. Battalion moves at 7.30.P.M. to same trenches as before. Capt. P. Wood awarded D.S.O for conspicuous gallantry on May 23d

Date time Place	Summary of Events & Information	Remarks
	at Sanctuary Wood in rallying troops under heavy shell & bomb fire, and in holding onto a trench after the order for retirement had been given. Lieut. W.N.J. Moore detailed for instruction in Adjutant's duties and attached to the first Duke of Cornwall L.I.	
July 9th	R.E. fired German sap in front of D 4 trench supported by rapid fire. Germans replied with rapid fire & whizz bangs. There were no casualties.	
July 10th Dettingen Huts. Dranoutre	Battalion returned to Dettingen Huts for rest. Parades & inspections carried on as usual. Working parties supplied for R.E's.	
July 14th	Battalion again takes over trenches D 1, D 2 & S.P. 5.	
July 17th 7.25 P.M	The Battalion marched on the night of the 17th & 18th July to Billets in Armentieres, quartered at Flax Factory.	
July 21st	The following Officers having reported their arrival were posted as follows:—	
ARMENTIERES	A. Coy. Capt. A.B. Hill, & II Lieut. Carrington B. Coy. II Lieut. Mullen & Baird. C. Coy. II Lieut. Bagley, Fry, Grantley-Smith, Voigt. D. Coy. II Lieut. Leighton & Brown.	

Date Hour Place	Summary of Events & Information	Remarks
July 22nd ARMENTIERES	Court of Enquiry held to enquire into the reason why a number of iron rations became unserviceable & deficient. President. Capt. W. Marley. Members. Lieut. Inskip. 2nd Lt. Carrington. The new Draft of Officers was lectured by the Medical Officer.	
July 23rd	The Commanding Officer wishes to express his appreciation of the gallant conduct of Capt. R.T.B. Glasspool & Lieut. J.A.N. Hessler who on the morning of the 20th rescued from drowning Pte. Gibson of B. Coy.	
July 24th 8.15 PM	Battalion proceeded to take over trenches 76, 77, 78 & S.P.Z. at L'Epinette. The allotment of trenches was as follows. A. Coy. 77 & S.P.Z. B. Coy. 78 & S.P.78. C. Coy. 76. D. Coy. 77 & 76. S.	
July 30th L'EPINETTE	C Coy was relieved by D & took over S.P.Z., S.P. 76, 77 & 78. While in these trenches working parties & Officers patrols were sent out. During one of these a German flag was captured by Capt. W. Marley.	

150th Inf.Bde.
50th Div.

1/5th BATTN. THE DURHAM LIGHT INFANTRY.

A U G U S T

1 9 1 5

1/5th Battalion The Durham Light Infantry.

August 1915

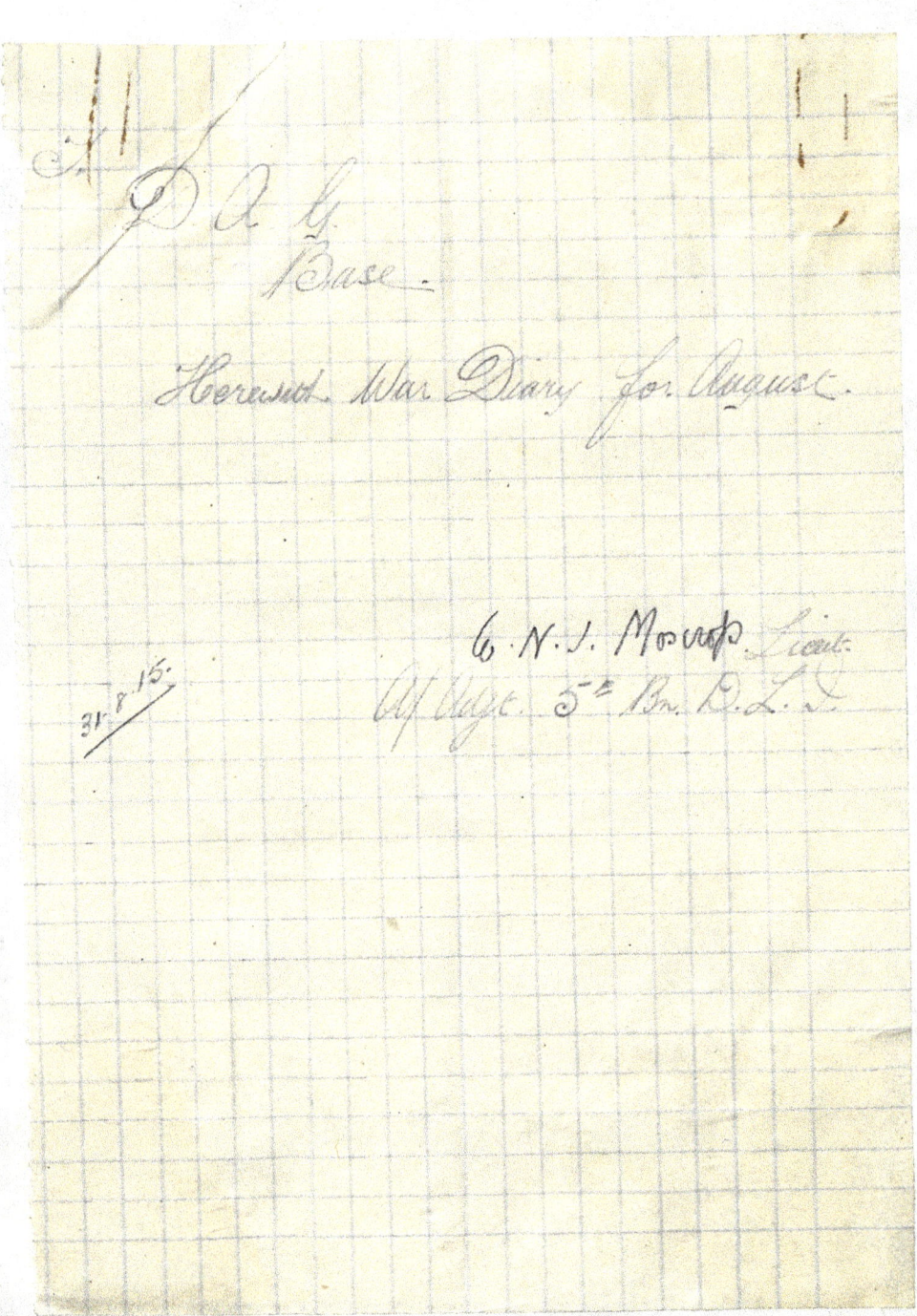

D.A.G.
Base

Herewith War Diary for August.

G. N. J. Mowrop Lieut.
A/Adjt. 5th Bn. D.L.I.

31·8·15

Time Place Date	Summary of Events & Information	Remarks
Aug. 1 to 4 L'EPINNETTE TRENCHES	2nd Lieut. Bagley slightly wounded in the foot, while censoring letters in his dug out. Generally speaking the trenches were quiet, but number 76 was much troubled with rifle grenades & bombs, while the parapets were continually being blown in with whizz-bangs. Owing to the energy of Captain Wilson & O Hessler and the willingness of the men the damage was soon repaired. During this time the Commanding Officer was on leave, & the Battalion was commanded by Captain A. L. Raimes.	
Aug. 4th	The Battalion was relieved by the 5th Yorkshire Regiment, but C Coy provided garrison for points S.P.Z & S.P.Y. These were under 2 Lieut Joy & Ward who were relieved on Aug. 6th. The Battalion less C Coy returned to Billets subsects & was billeted at the Asylum ARMENTIERES.	

Time. Place. Date.	Summary of Events & Information.	Remarks.
Aug. 7th ARMENTIERES	The Battalion moved out of billets at the Asylum into rest at ARMENTIERES & were again billeted at the Flour Factory.	
Aug. 8th	Divine Service Parade.	
Aug. 9th	Early morning running parade and parades under Coy. arrangements.	
Aug. 10th	Early morning parade, five mile route march in morning. 6 Officers & N.C.O's detailed for instruction in wiring & trench digging at the Asylum under Capt. Stowell R.E.	
Aug. 11th	Parades as before, R.E. course continued. Bathing parade at PONT. NIEPPE in afternoon.	
Aug. 12th	Early morning parade, Route march & bathing parades. O.C. Coys. went up in the morning to view trenches.	
Aug. 13th 7.45 P.M.	Battalion moves to the trenches as follows:- & took over from 5th North. Fusiliers & 5th Border Regt. A. Coy. 71 & 71 S. D. Coy. 72 & 72 S. B. & C. (O.C. Capt. Wilson) 73 & 73 S.	
Aug. 14th – 16th	Battalion in trenches, situation during the whole of this time.	

Time Place Date	Summary of Information & Events	Remarks
	was very quiet. Weather was bad in many cases trenches were flooded and parapets fell in. The Battalion during these few days were under the command of Capt. A.L. Raimes, the C.O. Lieut Col. G.O. Spence reporting sick & being sent down to ROUEN.	
Aug. 16th ARMENTIÈRES	The Battalion, less 50 men under 2nd Lieut. Mullen who remained to garrison LILLE POST, was relieved between 9 P.M. & 1 A.M. by the 4th YORKS. Regiment. B. Coy. were very late in being relieved owing to absence of guides. Returned to close supports at School in RUE LILLE, ARMENTIÈRES.	
Aug. 17th -19th	Battalion remained in Billets, & supplied working parties at night.	
Aug. 19th	Battalion returned to trenches & takes over Nos. 67 & 68. The distribution of Coys. was as follows:— A. Coy. (Capt. Hill) 67. B. Coy. (Capt. Marley) 67.S. C. Coy. (Capt. Wilson) 68. D. Coy. (Capt. Glasspool) 68.S.	

Time Place Date	Summary of Information & Events.	Remarks.
Aug. 19th ARMENTIÈRES	Capt. W.T. Wilkinson D.S.O. Adjutant 4th E. YORKS. takes over Command of Battalion (temporarily) Major. H. Ensor returns to duty from sick leave in England.	
Aug. 20th to Aug. 25th	Battalion in trenches, fatigue parties & working parties found by Coys. in support. During this tour in the trenches the enemy was extremely quiet there being practically no shelling at all, and until the last day, when several rifle grenades were put over 68 S., there were no casualties, but on this day there were two men wounded. Work done in trenches was as follows:- Constructing new trench near CHARD FARM. Conversion of trench into a traversed fire trench. Construction of a machine gun emplacement. Improvement of trench round buildings at LILLE POST. Construction of slits in communication trench. At this date home leave was cancelled temporarily, but to everyones relief it commenced again in a day	

TRENCHES 67 & 68. CHAPELLE ARMENTIÈRES.

Time, Place, Date	Summary of Information & Events	Remarks
Aug. 25th 9–10 P.M.	in two's time. The Battalion was relieved between 9 & 11 P.M. as follows. 67 & 67 S were taken over by the 8th D.L.I. who also found a garrison for LILLE POST. No. 68 & 68 S were relieved by the 5th LOYAL NORTH LANCS. The Battalion returned to ARMENTIÈRES and reoccupied its old Billets at the BLUE FACTORY in the RUE JULES LEBLEU.	
Aug. 26th ARMENTIÈRES	Time table was as follows:— Reveille . 6.30 A.M. Rouse Parade. 7.15. A.M. Breakfast. 8.0 A.M. Orderly Room. 9.0 A.M. Coys. paraded at 11. AM for rifle inspection by O.C. Coys. At 2.15 P.M. men had use of the Baths at PONT DE NIEPPE. 10% of the men were allowed out on pass from 2 PM to 8 P.M.	

Time. Place. Date.	Summary of Events & Information.	Remarks.
Aug. 27th.	Early morning running parades followed by Inspection & drill under Coy. arrangements. The Commanding Officer inspected A. Coy.	
Aug. 28th.	Battalion inspected by Army Commander. Sir Herbert Plummer. K.C.B. paraded in clean fatigue dress. After inspection Coy. went for a five mile route march & halted on getting back. Capt. A.L. Raimes assumed command of A. Coy. & Capt. P. Wood. D.S.O. resumed duties with "C" Coy.	
Aug. 29th.	Church Parade was held this morning. The undermentioned Officers having reported their arrival were posted temporarily for instruction to the following Coys. 2nd Lieut. Hunt. to. C. Coy. " " Empson. to D. Coy. Lt. W.N.S. Moncrieff acted as Adjutant in the absence of Capt. V.F. Gloag.	

Time Place Date	Summary of Events & Information	Remarks

Aug. 30th. At 6.30 A.M. the Battalion went for a Route March through ERQUINGHAM-LE-LYS and PONT-DE-NIEPPE. getting in about 9. A.M.
At 11.45 an inspection of clothing was held by the C.O.

Aug. 31st. 8.P.M. Battalion moves into Brigade Reserve at the Asylum ARMENTIÈRES. and provides two garrisons for Supporting points Y & Z. consisting of 40 men of A Coy under 2nd Lieut. Carrington and 40 men of C Coy under 2nd Lieut Polge. These two Officers were sent on ahead to reconnoitre the approach to these points.
2nd Lieut Brown attached to 1st Field Coy. R.E during the Battalions tour of duty in the trenches.
Strength on moving into reserve was.
  Officers. 23.
 Other Ranks. 519.

150th Inf.Bde.
50th Div.

1/5th BATTN. THE DURHAM LIGHT INFANTRY.

S E P T E M B E R

1 9 1 5

1/5th Battalion The Durham Light Infantry.

September 1915

Time Place Date	Summary of Events - Information.	Remarks
Sept 1st ASYLUM. ARMENTIERES	Upon arrival the previous night at the Asylum, the 5th Loyal North Lancs Regiment were found to be in occupation of some of our Billets. The change was made eventually without very much bloodshed. Parade in morning was as follows. Battalion taken in manual Drill by the Sergt. Major, a separate class being held for N.C.O's later in the morning. A signing class was held for N.C.O's & Officers under instruction of the R.E. M.G.'s & Bombers worked on their usual programme. Arrangements were made for Bathing the men. In the evening working Parties as under were found:—	
Sept. 2nd	2nd Lieut. Mullan admitted to Hospital. Lieut Davies returned from Hospital but unfit for duty. Coy. Officers allotted trenches in sector 74-75 & went up in morning to view them. Bombing & M.G. Officer likewise. Lt. Townsend & 5 Bombers attached to Divisional Grenade School for instruction. Working parties supplied as before.	

41

42

Time Place Date	Summary of Events & Information	Remark
Sept. 3d	The Battalion relieved the 5th YORKS. REGT. in trenches 74 & 75 & supports.	
ASYLUM. ARMENTIERES	The garrison of trenches was as follows 74. B. Coy. S.74 & S.S.74. 75. D Coy + 1 platoon C, S.75 C (less 1 Platoon)	
7.30 P.M	Garrisons of S.P.Y & S.P.Z were relieved by parties of the 5th YORKS & rejoined their Coys.	
Sept. 3d 5 Sept 12th	Battalion occupied the above named trenches in PLANK AVENUE during these days, & generally speaking the situation was quiet the whole time. Working parties were employed a great deal every day, making a new support trench & at the entrenchment behind 76.	
Sept. 12th ARMENTIERES	The Battalion was relieved about 7.30 P.M by the 7th & 8th D.L.I. on reaching ARMENTIERES. new billets were occupied in the Rue Sadi Carnot & Rue De Lille. Battalion Headquarters being at 66 RUE DE LILLE.	
Sept. 13th	Battalion inspected on Battalion alarm Post by G.O.C. York & Durham Infy. Brigade.	

43

Time. Date. Place	Summary of events & Information.	Remarks

ARMENTIERES

Sept. 14th — Coys. available for by. Officers. Battalion supplied a working party of 200 men under Capt. Hill. — in the morning under Capt. Marley.

Sept. 15th — The Battalion was inspected by G.O.C. 50th Division General Wilkinson.

On the night of 18/19th the Battalion took over trenches 72 & 73. The distribution of Coys. was as follows: —

7.20 P.M.
18th Sept.
72. C Coy + 30 men D Coy under Lieut. Simpson.
73. A Coy + 20 men " " " Lieut. Brown.
S.72 & S.73. B Coy under Capt. Marley.
Subsidiary Line remainder D Coy.

Trenches. 72 & 73.
Sept 19th — Morning spent in repairing B.H. marks. S.A.A. from these marks, & in practising men in returning to alt. trenches.
G.O.C. 50th Division drew attention to cases of looting in the town & the seriousness of the offences.

Sept 21st — Lieut C. Woods went on leave. The Division tries to brighten up our spare hours by succumbing to fashions call, and starting a Cinematograph Performance at the École Professionelle ARMENTIERES during the week.

Time, Date, Place	Summary of events & Information	Remarks
22nd Sept.	Divisional Orders issued to the effect that all shells or fuzes must not be dug up until examined by an Artillery Officer in order to facilitate location of enemy guns.	
23rd Sept.	Observation posts built behind 72 & 73 S. These were occupied throughout the day by an Officer armed with glasses & telescope. The posts were not of the best as they unfortunately had a habit of attracting "whizz bangs" & small "crumps". In the case of one which was used as chimney, one certainly accumulated soot, if not much information.	
24th	One Sergt & two men whose time had expired proceeded to permanent H Qrs. for transmission to the Base.	
25th	A general attack was carried out by French & English north & south of ARMENTIERES. The roll played by this Division was to demonstrate & lead the enemy to think that an attack was going to be delivered on this front. The previous night saw	

Time. Place. Date.	Summary of Events & Information	Remarks.

were dug out and a narrow forward trench dug about six feet in front of our parapet. In front of this ditch bundles of straw saturated with paraffin were placed. At 4.56 AM these bundles were to be lighted by men creeping out through the wire armed with boxes of matches. In some cases this was done, but the enemy who had already got the "wind up", saved us the trouble by sending "whizz bangs" into the straw and setting it alight. For the next hour or two our support lines were shelled & "whizz banged" after which things were quiet on our immediate front, but the heavy bombardment which had been going on for about a week previously continued intermittently. At the same time we were prepared for a move forward in case the enemy evacuated their trenches.

26th This being a Sunday we little expected a noisy day, but

Time/Place/Date	Summary of Events & Information	Remarks
March 7 & 8. Sept. 26th	The only signs of movement were in the village of Perenchies (PÉRENCHIES) opposite, where the Germans living up no doubt to their reputation of "Kulturists" were to be seen chasing some fair damsels about. Lieut. Wilkinson goes on leave.	
Sept 27th	Order issued to O.C. Coys. from G.O.C. 2nd Army that particular attention be paid to March Discipline & Saluting of Officers.	
28.	Reinforcements arrived & were split up amongst Companies. Capt. J.A.N. Hershew proceeded to the Base on temporary base duty for a month.	
Sept. 28th	The Commander in Chief draws attention to the prevalence of the offence of "Sleeping on Post" & that in future the extreme penalty will be awarded.	
Sept. 29th	The Commanding Officer regrets to announce the death of Pte. Stephenson No. 2320 A Coy. in Casualty Clearing Station BAILLEUL.	

150th Inf.Bde.
50th Div.

1/5th BATTN. THE DURHAM LIGHT INFANTRY.

O C T O B E R

1 9 1 5

1/5th Battalion The Durham Light Infantry.

October 1915

Time Place Date	Summary of Events & Information	Remarks
Oct. 3rd	2nd Lieut. E. Pope seriously wounded whilst observing from the front of 73 trench.	
Oct. 4th 7.30 P.M.	The Battalion during its stay in these trenches had Officers & men of the 9th LOYAL LANCS. attached to them for instruction & on the night of the 4th was relieved by the 4th YORKS & some Coys of the LANCS. On being relieved the Battalion proceeded to the ASYLUM. Two Officers and 80 other ranks of D Coy furnished garrison at LILLE POST.	
Oct. 5th ASYLUM ARMENTIERES	One platoon per Coy except D Coy detailed as inlying picquet. Routine. Reveille 6. A.M. Roll Call 6.45. Breakfast 7. Office Hour 9.30. Men had baths & a change of clothing & the usual inspections carried out. LILLE POST. garrison was relieved by two Officers & 80 men of C. Coy. at 7 P.M. Lieut Leighton went on leave.	

48

Time Place date	Summary of Events & Information	Remarks
Oct. 5th	Parades:- 10 to 11 A.M. Platoon drill under Platoon Commanders with special attention paid to handling of arms. Reinforcement men paraded at 10 a.m. under the Battalion Sergt. Major for Drill & Musketry Instruction. 11.30 to 12.30. Colparls parade under Sergt. Major. D. Coy men bathed.	
Oct. 6th	Parades:- Coys were under Coy. Officers for inspection & preparation for going to trenches.	
Oct. 7th 7 P.M. trenches 67 & 68.	The Battalion proceeded to relieve the 4th E. Yorks. Regiment in trenches 67 & 68. Distribution of Coys as follows. 67. B. Coy. 67.s. A. Coy. 68. D Coy. 68 s. C Coy. +1 Platoon C. Coy. LILLE POST. garrison relieved at 8.30 P.M. by 2 platoons of 4th E YORKS.	
Oct. 8th	Coys in support trenches supplied digging parties from 6.30 P.m to 12.30. A.M. These were engaged	

Time Date Place.	Summary of Events & Information	Remarks.
	in digging a sunk ditch for placing a hidden wire entanglement in	
Oct. 9th Oct. 12th	Platoons & Officers of the 14th Durham L.I. attached for instruction in trench warfare. Digging continued in front of trenches.	
Oct. 13th	The Artillery bombarded the enemy's wire and various points on the line north of L'EPINETTE. At the same time smoke bombs were let off from trench 71 onwards to 86. Men were withdrawn into shell trenches for safety, but made very little reply over this sector.	
Oct. 14th	This afternoon the Artillery bombarded for 40 minutes but the enemy made practically no reply. At 6.0 P.M the Battalion was relieved by the 5th Yorkshire Regiment & returned to Billets in ARMENTIERES. During the last tour in the trenches casualties were as follow. Killed 1. Wounded. 2.	

Time Date Place	Summary of Events & Information
Oct. 15th ARMENTIERES	At 8.45 A.M. troops were paraded in the cellars of their billets for practice in case of bombardment. This was followed by inspection of rifles & bayonets. Bathing parade at the Asylum. 20% of the men allowed out in the town on pass.
Oct. 16th Trenches 71-73. 5.45. P.M.	The Battalion moved into trenches & was distributed as follows:— A. Coy. 73 & 73.S. B. Coy. 71 & 71.S. C. Coy. 72 & 72.S. + 2 Platoons of 10th Yorks. D. Coy. Remained behind in ARMENTIERES & came up on the night of the 18th. Capt. Wilson sick & Capt. P. Wood, D.S.O. takes over command of "C" Coy. The Battalion relieved the 4th E. Yorks. Reg.
Oct. 16th to 22nd	In trenches, platoons of Kitchener Army. 10th Yorks, kept coming & going. This tour in trenches was particularly quiet & peaceful. Work:— All our energies were reserved for continuing the digging of the forward drain ditch as before. This was got well on.

Time Date Place	Summary of Events & Information.	Remarks.
	with. In the digging of it we were unfortunate enough to have two casualties through the earth giving way & burying the men. On the night of the 22nd/23rd we were relieved by the 5th Yorkshire Regt. & returned to our old billets in ARMENTIERES.	
Oct. 23d. ARMENTIERES	Coys. at disposal of O.C. Coys for inspections, Smoke Helmet Drill etc. A & D Coys. confined to billets being in Divisional Reserve.	
Oct. 24th.	Battalion Church Parade in National Schools Rue de Lille. Coys. preparing to go up to trenches 69 & 70 to relieve 4th E. YORKS. REGT. Battalion proceeded to trenches.	
Oct. 24th. – 29th.	In trenches 69 & 70 the Coys. being distributed as follows:- A Coy. 67 S. B " 67 (Right Sector) C " 67 (Left Sector) D " 70.	

Time, Date, Period	Summary of Events & Information	Remarks
Oct. 25th - 29th	During this tour we had no casualties but the weather was extremely bad with incessant rain, causing most of the parapet & parados to fall in particularly in the mushrooms. Coy. in fire trench had platoons of the 12th W. YORKS. REGT. in for instruction, and on the night of the 30th were relieved by them. In the afternoon the Artillery tried to get on to a gun which had been located in the woods near WEZ MACQUART. but were unable to get onto their Battery.	
Oct. 30th	On the night of the 30th the Battalion was relieved by the 5th YORKS. and the 12th WEST YORKS. attached to us. We returned to our old Billets in Armentières.	
Oct. 31st	B & C. Coys in Reserve confined to Billets - Bathing parade & kit inspections.	

150th Inf.Bde.
50th Div.

1/5th BATTN. THE DURHAM LIGHT INFANTRY.

N O V E M B E R

1 9 1 5

1/5th Battalion The Durham Light Infantry.

November 1915

53

Time Date Place	Summary of Events & Information	Remarks
Nov. 1st. ARMENTIERES.	Coy. at disposal of Coy. Officers. Went up at night to trenches 67 & 68. Where we had attached to us a 2 Coy. of the WEST YORKSHIRE REGT. During this tour which was a very quiet one, the weather was extremely bad, and it took us all our time to keep the parapets & parados up and the communication trenches passable for traffic. Capt. Cobrun went on leave and Capt. P. Woods took over command of the Coy. We were relieved on the night of the 7th November by the 5th YORKS. REGT. and returned to our old Billets in ARMENTIERES.	
Nov. 8, 9, 10.	Battalion in billets, time occupied by usual inspections Etc. On the night of the 9th Battalion returned to trenches 71, 72 & 73 for 48 hours. C Coy. remained down in reserve & was billeted at Ecole Jeanne D'Arc. This Coy. proceeded to trench 73 on the night of the 10th for 24 hours & relieved D. Coy. 10th. YORK & LANCS.	

Time Date Place	Summary of Events & Information	Remarks
Nov. 10th	Lieut. Col. Wilkinson K.O.S.B. taken away from us much to everyone's regret, and given command of the 4th EAST YORKS. REGT. Major H. Emson appointed to temporary command of 5th Durham L.I. in the absence of Lieut. Col. G.O. Spence.	
Nov. 11th	On the night of the 11th the Battalion returned to Billets in ARMENTIERES preparatory to moving back with the 50th Division on the following day. During the past day or two there was a marked increase in Artillery activity on the enemy's part. Our Battalion was relieved in the trenches by the 8th Somerset L.I.	
Nov. 12th	Battalion left ARMENTIERES at 9.30 A.M. Coys moving off at 10 minutes intervals & marched via PONT NIEPPE & BAILLEUL to Billeting area near OUTERSTEEN, arriving at 2.30 P.M. Men marched extremely well considering that with the exception of going to & from trenches no marching had been done for two or three months.	
Nov. 13th	Battalion at rest. Coys available for Coy inspections.	

TIME. PLACE. DATE.	Summary of Events & Information	
Nov. 14th	Church Parade on Battalion Alarm Post. Much amusement caused by the Padre's detached air and the Medical Officer's new Field Boots.	
Nov. 15th to Nov. 17th	Battalion commenced its programme of training to be carried out whilst the Division is at rest. 7 AM to 7.45 — Running Drill. 9 AM to 9.45 — Squad Drill. 10 to 11.0 AM — Manual, Musketry & Squad. 11.15 to 12.30 PM — Route March. 2 PM to 3 PM — Rifle exercises & Squad drill. and instruction in use of Tube Helmets. Battalion parade on alarm post for practise.	OUTTERSTEEN
	Nov. 18th. Squad drill and a short Route March.	
Nov. 19th	Battalion inspected at Head Quarters by G.O.C. 150. INFY. BRIGADE. Rest of day occupied by usual programme of work.	
Nov. 20th	Squad drill & Tube Helmet practise. "C" Day inspected by Major Emson.	
Nov. 21st	Sunday Church Parade followed by inspection of A & B. Coys by Major Emson, and issue of pay & clothing to Coys.	

Time Place Date	Summary of Events & Information.	Remarks.

Nov. 22nd — Battalion inspected by Brigadier General Bush who expressed his satisfaction at the turn out. Coys. were trained as per programme. In the afternoon there was a practice march past in preparation for the General inspection next day.

Nov. 23d — York & Durham Infy. Brigade inspected on a Route march by Lieut. General Sir. Herbert. D. Plummer. commanding 2nd Army. Route:— via BAILLEUL Rd. to OULTERSTEEN. then home by MERRIS. In the evening an alarm parade was held. message sent out at 7.55 P.M. Battalion ready to move off at 8.20 P.M.

OULTERSTEEN

Nov. 24 — Coy. training, special attention being paid to the practising of Artillery Formation.

Nov. 25th — Battalion Route march, round by METEREN & STRAZEELE. 7½ miles time taken 3½ hours. only two men fell out.

Nov. 26th — Battalion bathing parades & Coy training. In the evening a Concert was given in A Coys. barn got up by Capt. Robson, our versatile transport officer.

56

To. W.E.W.   57

When first of all you came to us we all were rather piqued.
Commanded by a Captain from a regiment never breeked.
At least we thought their knees were bare – all this beside the mark,
But can you wonder at us if we felt a grain of nark?

In vain we fanned our feelings and we locked our wounded pride
You pulled our leg to cheer us and you pulled our leg to chide,
And we soon were laughing with you save when work was left undone
And then we wholly failed to see the reason for your fun.

You taught us how to do the work the wherefore & the whens
And how to treat our Officers our N.C.O's and men
And how to soldier properly and how to cheer the hearts.
Of th' Dustly Durhams minus when entrenched in Flemish clarts.

But now alas you've left us to rejoin the 4th East Yorks.
We'd dearly love to have you back and all the little talks
We had on men and fishing and on Hunts and Hunting pink.
And we wish you every one of us all luck and every shot.

                          R.T.B.G.
                          Nov. 1915.

Nov. 27th Coys." did a Route March under Coy. arrangements & in the afternoon the football competitions were continued. Batt'n. Scouts were organized and attended lectures by Major Batty of the Divisional Staff.

Time. Date. Place.	Summary of Events & Information.	Remarks.
Nov. 28th	Divine Services in field at A.Coy. F.Hds. Coy Officers viewed trenches in preparation for practice attacks.	
Nov. 29th	Company training & Kit inspections. Intelligence Lecture given by Major Battys at BAILLEUL which Battn. Scouts attended.	
Nov. 30th	Battalion Route march via STRAZEELE, MERRIS & OUTTERSTEENE. Major Damm of the Bedfordshire Regt. ~~promoted~~ appointed to temporary command of the 5th Durham. L.I.	

OUTTERSTEENE

150th Inf.Bde.
50th Div.

1/5th BATTN. THE DURHAM LIGHT INFANTRY.

D E C E M B E R

1 9 1 5

Army Form C. 2118

WAR DIARY of the 5 Bn DURHAM L.I.
or
INTELLIGENCE SUMMARY December, 1915.
(Erase heading not required.)

Place	Date	Hour	Summary of Events and Information	Remarks and references to Appendices
OUTTERSTEENE	Dec 1st		Coys continued with the training & musketry on the attack, no further lectures by Major BATTYE. of the 50th Division on the use of the Rifle Grenade and the Lewis Machine attachment. Rumours dug in field near OUTTERSTEENE village. Coys did this in about 1½ hours intervals in the following order. A.C.B & D. The ground was bone dry in parts & going very heavy. Coy. did very well, & the Divisional & Brigade Staffs who were present remarked especially well this. The Brigadier was particularly pleased with the manner in which B. Coy. who had mainly carried out the attack. The Bombing partie was particularly good and the officer commanding them mentioned Coy. was of the animals of the Coy Commander for the surrounding of the day.	
	Dec 3.		Very wet and practically no field work done. Coys returned in Billets under by arrangements.	
	Dec 4	9 A.M.	Battalion route march, continued with a tactical exploration on Battn & Brigade Alarm Posts. Route taken OUTTERSTEEN village cross railway towards DOULIEU then along BAILLEUL roads to main BAILLEUL — MERRIS roads, & home by CAPBANK En[?].	
	Dec 5		Church Parades on A. Coy. Parade ground. In the afternoon the final of the Battalion football competition was played between the Transport and No 3 Watson of A. Coy. Run off. A. Coy. goal. Transport N.K. Medals were presented by the winning team by Major Crosby.	

WAR DIARY of the 5th DURHAM. L.I.
INTELLIGENCE SUMMARY for December, 1915

Place: OUTTERSTEENE

Date	Hour	Summary of Events and Information	Remarks
Dec. 6th		but weather still continues very protracted the attack over the open & the use of Tube H.Bombs. Special course of instruction continued for M.G's, Bombers & Scouts. Lieut W. Y.O. Spencer returned from sick leave & was assumed command of the Battalion.	
Dec. 7th	8.50 AM	Battalion paraded for a route march thro' STRAAZEEL, MERRIS & OUTTERSTEEN.	
Dec. 8th		Coys. at disposal of O.C. Coys. for leg training & bombing instruction.	
Dec. 9th	9.20 AM	Route march under Brigade arrangements in following order: 4th E.YORKS, 4th E.YORKS, 5th D.L.I. handed over Brigade Maxim Pat- at OUTTERSTEEN at 9 A.M. & moved off at 9.20. Route:— BAILLEUL road to CLAPBANK up through NOOT-BOOM to STRAAZEELE. The weather was extremely trying & after reaching 4th E.YORKS. H.Q. Battalions were dismissed to Billets.	
Dec. 10th		Coys. at disposal of O.C. Coys. for leg training. Specialists worked with usual courses	
Dec. 11th		Inspection of Battalion by commanding Officer, cols. awing to weather the men to be unduerkhaki	
Dec. 12th		Church Parade on A. Coy. Parade ground.	
Dec. 13th		Coys. were inspected by the commanding Officer at Coy. Bills. Lieut. V.F. King attended a staff Tour of the 50th Division agent is 2nd A.H.Q. The Billeting Officer of the 10th ARGYLES came through to inspect billets for his Regiment which we alone.	
Dec. 14th		Bathing parade in the afternoon returned. Advance party of 16 men under Lieut. Townsend moved to DICKEBUSH hut to take over	

WAR DIARY of the 5th DURHAM L.I.

INTELLIGENCE SUMMARY   December 1915

Army Form C. 2118

Place	Date	Hour	Summary of Events and Information	Remarks and references to Appendices
—	Dec. 15th		OUTTERSTEEN. In afternoon O.C. Coys & Scouts attended a lecture by Capt. Cornwall of the 2nd Army on the system of enemy Photographic At 5.0 p.m. O.C. Coys was instructed on the system of identifying troops in the field. In the evening a concert got up by Capt. Roberson was held in H.Q's. Billet.	
—	Dec. 16th		Coy training including a route march. Tube Helmet drill. In the afternoon the Battalion played Bn. 5th Northumberland Fus Siers at A.Coys. ground. Result 2 goals each.	
—	Dec. 17th		Coy training under Coy arrangements.	
—	Dec. 18th		Coy training & general preparations for move.	
—	Dec. 19th		Church Parade.	
—	Dec. 20th	9.20 A.M.	Battalion paraded on Battn. alarm post and moved off at 9.30 A.M. to STEENWERKE station where it entrained at 1.30 p.m. for POPERINGHE where it detrained and marched to DICKEBUSH Huts arriving at 7 p.m.	
	Dec. 21		Troops rested in Huts. Lng. Officers, M.G. & Bombing Officers went up to view trenches A.3 – A.6. @ Vulbart Road – R.1. at present held by 4th YORKS. REGT.	
	Dec. 22		Weather was very bad & kept a better command in huts. Time a head in writing & Preparing for trenches	
DICKEBUSH Huts.	Dec. 23.	1–2 p.m.	Battalion paraded ten tenches & marched via DICKEBUSH KRUISSTRAAT @ ZILLEBEKE & relieved the 4th YORKS	

WAR DIARY of the 5th DURHAM L.I.
or INTELLIGENCE SUMMARY for December, 1915

Army Form C. 2118

(Erase heading not required.)

Place	Date	Hour	Summary of Events and Information	Remarks and references to Appendices
TRENCHES. A3-A6. ARMAGH WOOD. YPRES.	Dec 24th to Dec 27th		Distribution of Coys was as follows. A3 & A4 - A Coy under Major Raimes. A5 & A6 - B Coy under Capt. Mosley. Strong point R.1 - C Coy under Capt. William D Coy under Capt. Glanshoed remained behind in reserve at "Scottish Lines" BUSSEBOOM. The 150th Brigade were the centre Brigade of the Division the D.L.I. Bgd. being on our left and the Northumberland Fusiliers on our right. The 5th D.L.I. held the left sub-sector of the centre Brigade. Battn in front line trenches generally speaking there was little activity on the sector. Artillery. A large number of "heavies" dropped in front of the left of our sub-sector. Christmas Eve & Christmas Day passed quietly but the hum of part guns was not noted. One Officer patrol under 2nd Lieut. E. John went out from French A.3. & found some Germans in the ruined farm in "No Man's Land" & threw a bomb into them which "dud" but the Germans were not enough to attack and he patrol returned safely. No observation had been had in these trenches until the Regiment went in. The scoutht men were embodied in the front line trenches by the Battalion scouts under the Scout N.C.O. Lieut W.P. for the Bn. part took two had from our walking Lieut. T.R.F. & 6 men wounded. & 3 men of A. Coy.	
RAILWAY DUG OUTS. 1.20.D.6.8.			On the night of the 27th the Battalion was relieved by the 4th YORKS. REGT. & on relief the Battalion went into Brigade Reserve in RAILWAY DUG OUTS Lieut Simpson & 58 men attached to the 175th Tunnelling Coy. R.E.	

WAR DIARY of the 5th DURHAM L.I. for December 1915.
or
INTELLIGENCE SUMMARY

Army Form C. 2118

(Erase heading not required.)

Place	Date	Hour	Summary of Events and Information	Remarks and references to Appendices
RAILWAY DUG OUTS.	Dec. 28th		Battalion at Railway dug outs, in relation of half Bn. carried out by exp. This Battalion were the only one in the 50th Division, which had not a single case of trench feet. This was largely due to the unceasing care & hard work of the M.O. Capt. H.F. WILKIN and of the Stretcher Bearer Officer nominated G.H.Q. area around ZILLEBECKE.	
	Dec. 29th 6.30 pm		D. Coy. relieved B. Coy in Railway Dug outs and B Coy moved back to SCOTTISH LINES BUSSEBOOM.	
	Dec. 30th		Battalion remained in Railway Dug outs.	
Trenches A3 - A6.	Dec. 31st 6.0 pm		B. Coy. moved away from "Sutherland Farm" to relieve the 5th Yorks at "St James Dug Outs" and the Battalion relieved the 4th Yorks. Regt. in trenches A.3 - A.6. Coys. lying as follows:— A coy. Strong point. R.1. C coy. A.3 × A.4. D coy. A.5 × A.6. During this tour D coy came in for half an hours bombardment of their trench but escaped rightly with two men wounded.	

signed W. Spence Lieut. Col.
Commanding 5th Durham L.I.

1/5th Durham L.I.

Jan
7.(VII

50

150 Bde

Army Form C. 2118

Instructions regarding War Diaries and Intelligence Summaries are contained in F.S. Regs., Part II. and the Staff Manual respectively. Title Pages will be prepared in manuscript.

WAR DIARY of 5th DURHAM. L.I.
or
INTELLIGENCE SUMMARY JANUARY. 1916.
(Erase heading not required.)

Place	Date	Hour	Summary of Events and Information	Remarks and references to Appendices
Trenches. A3–A6. ARMAGH WOOD.	JAN.1.	7.P.M.	The Battalion relieved the 4th YORKS. REGT. in trenches A3–A6. and during the four days of unusually fine situation remaining normal & quiet.	
DICKEBUSH HUTS.	JAN.4.	7-30 P.M.	Battalion relieved to Dickebusch where it remained for four days in Divisional Reserve.	
	Jan 5		Divine Service.	
	JAN.6.		Coy. Comdrs. & dispatched at O.C. Coys. ands for following parades. Extract from Operation Orders for moves from Dickebusch in case of attack:- A. Coy. 1 Platoon to FRENCH. HOUSE. (I.27.A.8.6.) " " " 1.A. (I.21.D.2.9.) A. Coy. remainder + B. to BEDFORD HOUSE. (I.26.C.9.9.) C. Coy. will occupy. S.H.Q 2nd line from BELGOED FARM to I.19.C.7.0. D. Coy. + H.Q. ovaling. 11.30.A. Extract from Operation Orders for moves from RAILWAY DUG OUTS. (3rd Reserve) in case of attack:- In the event of attack the Bn. will move to north of RUDKIN'S HOUSE. as follows:- A. Coy. in Trench not farm. B. " in E. end of dug outs. C. " in W. end of dug outs. Grenadier Platoon. M.G. Section.	
Trenches. A3–A6.	JAN.7th	2.45. 5. 3.30. P.M	Battalion relieved to trenches A3–A6. Having dis tributed as follows. A.3– A.4. C. Coy. under Capt. Wham A.5– A.6. D. Coy. " " Nelson Rork. R.I. B. Coy. " " Gray.	

Army Form C. 2118

WAR DIARY of 5th DURHAM. L.I.
or
INTELLIGENCE SUMMARY
January, 1916.

(Erase heading not required.)

Instructions regarding War Diaries and Intelligence Summaries are contained in F. S. Regs., Part II. and the Staff Manual respectively. Title Pages will be prepared in manuscript.

Place	Date	Hour	Summary of Events and Information	Remarks and references to Appendices
RAILWAY DUG. OUTS.	JAN. 11th		Battalion made fall into Brigade Reserve & remained here until the 15th when it returned to Trenches A.3 - A.6 relieving the 4th Yorks. Regt. While in dug outs we supplied working parties during morning & night of 300 men) to 1st & 2nd Field Coys. R.E.	
Trenches A.3 - A.6. R.I.	JAN. 15th		During the tour we had rather a rough time. Our artillery had an organised shoot which was followed by enemy retaliation & a shoot on their part. Our Trench Mortar Battery R.I. was bombarded for two hours with rounds of "crumps" & "larger. Heavy P's came in for a good shelling our working party for an hour. Major Raynor our Medical Officer Capt William and 2nd Lieut Major Wilkinson & Sergt Major [?] were killed. Sudden none of them were very serious and our total casualties only amounted to 2 men killed & 12 wounded.	
	JAN. 20th	7.0 P.M.	Battalion was relieved by 4th Yorks. Regt. and returned to DICKEBUSH. HUTS. When it arrived there was [?] and the usual inspection was carried out.	
	JAN. 24th		Batt. marched up to Trenches A.3 - A.6. When the whole of the Batt. were on relief — 2 Platoons A. Coy. remainder down at SCOTTISH. LINES. With Capt. P. Wood. D.S.O. Tr. A.3 - A.4 — C Coy + 2 Platoon A. Coy. A.5 - A.6. — D Coy + 2 Platoon B. Coy. S.P. R.I. Remainder B. Coy. 2nd Lieut (a) C.O. Shurus later own temporary command of 150th Brigade. Major A. Brown takes command of Battalion & much unwounded. Their Lieut. were [?] and unwounded. [?] & C.T.'s. mainly were down in F. Trenches	

Army Form C. 2118

WAR DIARY of 5th Batt. Durham. L.I.
or
INTELLIGENCE SUMMARY   January 1916

(Erase heading not required.)

Instructions regarding War Diaries and Intelligence Summaries are contained in F.S. Regs., Part II. and the Staff Manual respectively. Title Pages will be prepared in manuscript.

Place	Date	Hour	Summary of Events and Information	Remarks and references to Appendices
Tunnel A3 - A6	Jan. 26		Quiet day, mornings messages from Brigade at 11 p.m. ordering for stand (trenches) to readiness for possible Gas attack.	
Armagh Wood	Jan. 27	7.0 p.m.	Battn. relieved at 7 p.m. by 4th Yorks & returned to Bgd. Reserve in Railway Dug Outs. Capt. R.T.B. Glasspool unable to take up appointment, on our return to 2nd Army & Short of nursing at Mont. Des. Cats.	
	Jan. 29			
	Jan. 31	6 p.m.	2nd Lieut. Officers sent to trenches at Hill. 60. Nos. 37-45 & 01- 6 p.m. moved back to Scottish Lines. where it remained in Div. Reserve for during the month we had a draft of 30 men & four Officers from the 3d Bn. Some of these Lieut's Brown, Henlen & Butterfield were original officers who had been wounded on Whit. Monday. The Brigade M.G. took over & held trench to end of the month, and the Battalion sent Lieut. C. Wood, & J.N. Henlen, Sergt. Major Coomle & 20 men to this [?]. Honours & Awards mentioned in Field Marshall. Sir. J.D.P. French's despatch dated 30th Nov. 1915 for gallant and dis tinguished service in the field. (Acting. London Gazette. d/ 1-1-16.)	

WAR DIARY or INTELLIGENCE SUMMARY

Army Form C. 2118

of the 5th DURHAM L.I. for January 1916.

(Erase heading not required.)

Place	Date	Hour	Summary of Events and Information	Remarks and references to Appendices

Lieut Col. Shewan. C.O.
Revd. (Comb. Capt.) Gfraig. Y.F.
Capt. Watson. H.R.
Lieut. (Temp Capt.) Lumb. P. D.S.O.
2/Lieut. (Temp 2nd.) Marsh. W.N.J.
1312 Sgt. Brown N.E. } C. Coy
2274 " Miller J.   } C. Coy
2762 L/M. Comr T.   } C. Coy
2417 Pte. Bryant E.A. } A. Coy
1370 "   Clark W.   } B. Coy
3263 "   Jillleigh W.F.} C. Coy
                       } A. Coy
                       } C. Coy

In furtherance of the following awards were won by this Battalion.

Capt. H.R. Watson.   Military Cross
L/Capt. V.F. Young.   Military Cross
Battn. Sergt. Major. T. Russ
2228 Cpl. Jolly. C. Coy } Distinguished Conduct Medal
1433 L/Cpl. Eginton D. Coy }

Signed. Hewson. Major.
Commanding. 5th Durham L.I.

Army Form C. 2118

WAR DIARY of the 5th DURHAM.L.I.
or
INTELLIGENCE SUMMARY
(Erase heading not required.)

From 7 January 1916.

Instructions regarding War Diaries and Intelligence Summaries are contained in F.S. Regs., Part II. and the Staff Manual respectively. Title Pages will be prepared in manuscript.

Place	Date	Hour	Summary of Events and Information	Remarks and references to Appendices
SCOTTISH LINES	Jan 1st	9.30	Battalion at rest in huts. in the afternoon.	
		12.30	During the hours of five days not in programme of training. Paid down by the 50th Division. Shewbath carrels out. there was work	
BUSSEBOOM	Jan 2nd	7.15 – 7.45 A.M.	Bayonet fighting & Physical drill.	
		9.30 – 12.0	Platoon drill.	
		2.15 – 3.15 P.M.	Before, a short instruction & a possible enemy.	
	Jan 3rd		Battalion parade at POPERINGHE after which they were at disposal of Lay. Officer 2 Platoons of "C" Coy were marched to NORTHUMBERLAND LINES for loads under Lieut RUTHERFORD. Capt W.H. ROBSON attended Brigade horn show. Lieut RUTHERFORD appointed Regimental Transport Officer.	
	Jan 4th		Battalion attended Divisional Service in Y.M.C.A. Hut. In afternoon Coy training - Lectures were continued. Lieut. Col. G.O. SPENCE returned from Brigade & assumes command of the B battalion.	
	Jan 5th		Coy drill in morning, in the afternoon Lectures under Coy arrangements.	
	Jan 6th	2.45 P.M. 3.20 P.M.	Battalion moved off from SCOTTISH LINES - handed to trenches at HILL 60, where it relieved the 6th NORTHUMBERLAND FUSILIERS in trenches 37.L.6 48.R. inclusive, distribution of Coys was as follows	
			A. Coy. 38L Fan × 38 S. + 24 bombers	
			B. Coy. 39 × 39 S. + 24 "	
			C. Coy. 47×48 × 47,48 s. + 8 "	
			D. Coy. 37L 38 R × 316 + 4 "	
HILL.60			Regimental Dump at ZILLEBEKE STATION Dressing Station at RAILWAY CUTTING.	

Army Form C. 2118

WAR DIARY of the 5th DURHAM L.I.
or
INTELLIGENCE SUMMARY 7 January 1916
(Erase heading not required.)

Instructions regarding War Diaries and Intelligence Summaries are contained in F. S. Regs., Part II. and the Staff Manual respectively. Title Pages will be prepared in manuscript.

Place	Date	Hour	Summary of Events and Information	Remarks and references to Appendices
Trenches 37 L to 48 R Hill 60.	Feb 7th to Feb 13th		During our tour in the trenches we had a fairly quiet time, every howitzer battery of our chiefly behind 39, 40 & 41 S and continually worried us with trench mortars & rifle grenades for which trenches 37 & 38 seem in for unusually at minimum. The nights were unusually noisy & retaliation was severe. On the afternoon of the 13th the time of which enemy certainly at 2 p.m. their shells until 4 P.M. at which a bombardment opposite the G.B. (Gun Post commenced of a rather under which the summer attacked. Heavy enemy were seen to put up a heavy cloud working parties was continually being obtained damage to front trenches & making the new line behind 37 few trenches. The called upon 4th E. YORKS & 4th YORKS every night few there parties. During this time we had a heating of cable attacks to us for 48 hours retaliation in trench routine.	
	Feb 13th	8.30pm	On the night of the 13th-14th the Battalion were relieved by the 4th YORKS. REGT. & went into Brigade Reserve as follows: A. Coy. BLAUWE POORT FARM. I.27.B.53. B. Coy. SWAN CHATEAU. I.19.C.4.6. C. Coy. BEDFORD HOUSE. H.30.A. D. Coy. Dug outs at H.14.60.	
BEDFORD HOUSE. I.26.A.8.1.	14th		This day remained with a good deal of shelling which at 2.30pm onwards our trenches & gunners after bombarding trench 33 - 25 attacks the "Bluff" trenches then returning about 600 yds of trench. At the same time they retaliated attacks trenches by fierce by 2 platoons of 41 at H.14.60.	
		4.0 P.M.	Battalion ordered to stand by ready to concentrate if required.	
		7.40 P.M.	Orders to concentrate at BEDFORD HOUSE received.	
		8.40 P.M.	Concentration complete. Signed Henry [illegible] H C L I B	

Army Form C. 2118

WAR DIARY of 52 DURHAM. L.I.
or INTELLIGENCE SUMMARY
for January 1916
(Erase heading not required.)

Place	Date	Hour	Summary of Events and Information	Remarks and references to Appendices
BEDFORD HOUSE I.26.A.8.1	14th Jan.	8.40 p.m	C. Coy. & Bn. relieved by Bn 7th DURHAM. L.I. known Battalion.	
	15th		At 5.30. A.m. 2 minings were received announcing Coys. to return to Billets but Skinner took one rill to his dept garrie ends. Capt Upton went on leave & Capt. Hill took over command of C. Coy.	
	18th		Battalion Hd 16th & 18th was held fairly quiet day except for shelling activity on both sides, BEDFORD HOUSE & Township being shelled. Infantry enough to keep off. 3rd Single. A Coy. Sunny holding Trenches batter was shelled every night to 48 Yorks. Regt. who were [?] left day out. holding Trenches 37 & 5 a 8 R.	
		8.30 p.m	Bn was relieved on the night of 18/19 out the Bn 52 DURHAM L.I. & returned into Divisional RESERVE at SCOTTISH LINES.	
SCOTTISH LINES	19th		One casualties during the time. Trenches days war. 10 Killed, 36. wounded.	
BUSSEBOOM H.23.B.5.9.			Coys. at disposal of O.C. Coys. for own pictures and indiv indiv. Inspection the continuous of Officers was held at 9.30. A.m. in Officers Mess.	
	20th	9-10 A.m	Coys parade. Drin arm drill. distinguished, extending, an rendered & mounting Maxim carried at 11 A.m	
		2.30 3.30	Coys. at disposal of O.C. Coys for traininger & Skirmishet Cearture Officer Class under Lieut. Carrington in the [?] Room.	
	21st		Coys. Training. Battering Parades & Skirmish[?] [?]	

WAR DIARY of the 5th DURHAM. L.I.

or

INTELLIGENCE SUMMARY February 1916

Army Form C. 2118

(Erase heading not required.)

Place	Date	Hour	Summary of Events and Information	Remarks and references to Appendices
SCOTTISH LINES	22nd		Coy. was inspected by the Commanding Officer during the morning, and owing to the bad weather this was held in the huts. Battalion trench attack practice.	
	23rd		Battalion inspected on Coy. parade ground by Brig-General PRICE commanding 150th Brigade. No work was done owing to weather conditions.	
	24th	3-4 P.M.	Battalion moved to trenches A.4 - A.11. Heads Quarters + 30 men per Coy. taken over from the Anglican YPRES. by motor buses. 2' relieved the 7th NORTHUMBERLAND FUSILIERS. Distribution of Coys in trenches was as follows :- A. Coy. A4 + A5 B. Coy. A6 + A7 } The relief of the trenches was completed at 8.30 P.M, but owing to min understanding our Lewis guns were not in trenches C. Coy. A8 - A9 D. Coy. A10 - A11 } on final relief completed until 2 o'clock on the morning of the 25th	
Trenches A.4 - A.11 YPRES	26th		The 25th was quiet but weather was bad. Preparations commenced for the summer relief which the 50th Division were to deliver within the next few days. Extra rations, S.A.A. etc stored in trenches. Out own of intake on our immediate front was this afternoon now advanced rapidly when we were working. This was light under down construction and patrols were sent over to it every night. Preparations complete.	
	27th		Brigade is made up of one advance of the Battalion in trenches by which in Coy saw up. A.4 - A8 to the A.12 from the 5th YORKS. 4th YORKS. + Coys were	

Army Form C. 2118

WAR DIARY of the 5th DURHAM. L.I.
or
INTELLIGENCE SUMMARY   January, 1916.
(Erase heading not required.)

Instructions regarding War Diaries and Intelligence Summaries are contained in F.S. Regs., Part II. and the Staff Manual respectively. Title Pages will be prepared in manuscript.

5/

Place	Date	Hour	Summary of Events and Information	Remarks and references to Appendices
Trenches. A.9 – A.12.	27th		Battn. distribution was then as follows :- A. Coy. Strong points R.3 & R.4 & 30 mun in reserve line. B. Coy. Subsidiary & CUMBERLAND. Dug. Outs. (edge of SANCTUARY WOOD). C. Coy. + 20 mun @ Coy. A.9 & A.10. D. Coy. + 20 mun. A. Coy. A.11 & A.12.	
	28th & 29th		There was quiet day. work for artillery fire, which was directed chiefly against VIGO STR. communication Trench & reserve line near CUMBERLAND. Dug. Outs. B. Coy. losing 7 men at men in two later. Weather was bad. Rain & snow. Work done was running & improving rubber knee, drawing out leads and ground work in front line trench. Communication trench and reserve lines mended.	

(signature) E Reed
Lieut. Colonel.
Commanding 5th DURHAM. L.I.

Army Form C. 2118

WAR DIARY
or
INTELLIGENCE SUMMARY

of the 5th DURHAM. L.I. for MARCH, 1916.

(Erase heading not required.)

Instructions regarding War Diaries and Intelligence Summaries are contained in F. S. Regs., Part II. and the Staff Manual respectively. Title Pages will be prepared in manuscript.

Place	Date	Hour	Summary of Events and Information	Remarks and references to Appendices
Trenches A 9 - A.12. SANCTUARY WOOD	MARCH 1st		A quiet day until the evening when a bombardment was carried out on a D. nominal front from 5 to 5.45 p.m. consisting of 9.2" guns, 5" guns, rifle gren. It was intended to use a mohair bomb as a further aid to "putting the wind up" the Huns but the winds were not favourable. The bombardment seemed to succeed in its purpose of drawing enemy fire excellently and their artillery was remarkably quick in damaging the bottom of Vigo St. and along our SA ares line. At about 7.p.m. this situation became quieter & the night was peaceful.	
	2nd		There was this morning of our attack on the BLUFF further and in order to all. the 17th Division was again intimated and demonstration of the night before but on addition our trench mortars "hoffer" the B. Budings and we exploded two mines just in front of it. Enemy retaliated quickly as usual thrown in on the Minnens., might and others in a more friendly B.3. cold by the 5th YORKS causing cas. rather & doing damage to trenches. The day was taken up with settling for less time many an hour until nightfall.	
	3-5		Three days were extremely quiet- minny chilling to the weather which was snow, sleet a heavy snow. The trenches were deep in feet with water and owing to lack of dug outs the men had a roughish time	

Army Form C. 2118

WAR DIARY of the 5th DURHAM. L.I.

or

INTELLIGENCE SUMMARY
for MARCH. 1916.

(Erase heading not required.)

Place	Date	Hour	Summary of Events and Information	Remarks and references to Appendices
	9th	11.30 p.m.	fait suffered, but we obtained our second by rapid passage & single case of bomb fell at YPRES where it exploded by the 1st ROYAL FUSILIERS & wounded 5 H.H. central 1 Officer was killed in POPPERINGHE on reviewing hun at 3.A.M. many & Officer was killed in the RUE YPRES & RUE MESSINES.	
	10-11		No work done & men rested in Billets.	
	12th		One hour with under leg arrangements followed by Divine service in afternoon.	
POPPERINGHE	13th		leg carried out leg training and shields was taken on a hundred counter.	
	14th		Battn. marched from POPPERINGHE to DICKEBUSH HUTS camp a leaving in queue of an hour intervals first leg moving off at 4.45 p.m. hour visible leg 8 p.m.	
DICKEBUSH HUTS. A.	15th		leg following at POPPERINGHE & DICKEBUSH. In the morning. In the afternoon between a shield counter.	
	16th		On fire two 15th	
	17th		leg training and practising of bombing attacks on hands, and firing on the 200 yds. range.	
HILL 60.	18th		Battalion marched to trenches at HILL 60. occupying 37.L. to 40. and a shelter in rear. Division of leg. was as follows. A. leg. 40 & 40.s. B. leg. 39 & 39.s. C. leg. 38 & 38.s. D. leg. 37.L & 37.L. shelter	

Army Form C. 2118

WAR DIARY of 5th DURHAM. L.I.
or
INTELLIGENCE SUMMARY
for MARCH. 1916.

(Erase heading not required.)

Instructions regarding War Diaries and Intelligence Summaries are contained in F.S. Regs., Part II. and the Staff Manual respectively. Title Pages will be prepared in manuscript.

Place	Date	Hour	Summary of Events and Information	Remarks and references to Appendices
Trenches 37L6 40. Hill 60.	18th		Battalion relieved 8th DURHAM. L.I. relief complete at 10.P.M. On arrival we were greeted by the usual of a minute activity, the Heads quarters at the DUMP. The 19th was quiet except for minor activity, the Germans was heard working which 37. L. & R. killing four & wounding two of our own men. From the 19th to the 24th the situation was quiet as two as artillery activity was concerned, but mortars, trench mortars & rifle grenades worried us considerably.	
	24th		Battalion relieved by 7th NORTH FUSILIERS. The day was quiet until about 7 P.M. at which time enemy started an organized shoot lasting until 10 P.M. It extends our front line. Information having few got of our relief coming off. 37. L + 35 trenches came in for the worst of the shelling and the cutting for Trench mortars & "run away". After relief Bn. proceeded to SCOTTISH LINES. Casualties the past tour 12 killed, 15 wounded.	
25th & 31st SCOTTISH LINES.			Coy at disposal of O.C. Eng. for instruction and Bathing at POTERINGHE.	
BUSSEBOOM		11.30 A.M.	Church Parade at 11.30 A.M. in Y.M.C.A. Cml. & recruit draft in hutch to B.G.C. 150th Bgd.	
26th	28th		Battalion moved from SCOTTISH LINES to billeting area between ST. JEAN. CAPEL & BAILLEUL.	
28th	28th	5.30 A.M.	Route march on a Brigade and OUDERDOM, RENINGHELST, WESTOUTRE, MONT. NOIR, SHAXEN -	
	28th 31st		Coys. at disposal of O.C. Eng. for various fair. Kemmel	

W.S. [signature]
Lieut-Col.
Commanding 5th DURHAM. L.I.

5D

1/5 Durham L I

Vol X

WAR DIARY of the 5th DURHAM. L.I.

INTELLIGENCE SUMMARY

Army Form C. 2118

(Erase heading not required.)

April. 1916.

Instructions regarding War Diaries and Intelligence Summaries are contained in F.S. Regs., Part II. and the Staff Manual respectively. Title Pages will be prepared in manuscript.

Place	Date	Hour	Summary of Events and Information	Remarks and references to Appendices
BADAJOS HUTS. LOCRE.	April 1st		Battalion in Divisional reserve at LOCRE huts.	
	2nd		Church Parade in field behind huts & in afternoon O.C. Coys inspected billets at KEMMEL.	
G1 – H1A. Trenches at KEMMEL. Anker Brigade Ref: Substitu.	April 3rd to 7th		While in Divisional reserve at LOCRE Battalion available eight guards round KEMMEL & working parties to Battns. holding the front line. Lay hummy as few as hostile war carried on and rituals. Instruction given in flying wall, exercise in & bayonet fighting.	
	7th.	6-7 pm	Battalion moved to trenches at KEMMEL HILL and relieved the 4th YORKS. Regt. Disposition of Coys. as follows :—	
			G1 to C 3. A Coy + 2 Maxim D. Coy	
			G2 to H1A. B Coy + 2	
			S.P. 10 . C Coy. 2 Platoons	
			S.P. 11 . C Coy 1 "	
			Fort. SASCATCHWAN C Coy 1/2	
			REGINA. C Coy 1/2	
			Lieut Col. G.O. SPENCE was on Leave during the time and the Battalion was under the command of MAJOR H. ENSOR. Our first day here was quiet but in the next three we have been under "Canards" two & three times a day for a duration of 1/2 an hour. Casualties at 1st the 13th were	
			2 Officers wounded, viz. Major RAIMES & Capt. MARLEY	
			1. O.R. Killed	
			16. O.R. (wounded)	

WAR DIARY of the 5th DURHAM L.I.
INTELLIGENCE SUMMARY for April, 1916.

Army Form C. 2118

(Erase heading not required.)

Instructions regarding War Diaries and Intelligence Summaries are contained in F.S. Regs., Part II. and the Staff Manual respectively. Title Pages will be prepared in manuscript.

Place	Date	Hour	Summary of Events and Information	Remarks and references to Appendices
Trenches G1–H1A KEMMEL	April 12th	11 p.m.	On the right of the 12th a man of the 205th Bavarian Regt. was seen in front of our trenches abt G1. He was trying to get through our wire with the intention of surrendering. He was fired at & hit in two places slightly wounding his enemy own trenches. He was brought down to Bn. H.Qrs. & showed great cheerfulness & pleasure at being in our hands.	
	14th		Lieut. V.F. GIBBS our Bombing Officer was slightly wounded in the nose by 2 pieces of shell whilst looking at some work in the VIA GELLIA C.T. by our bombers to the advanced dressing station in KEMMEL VILLAGE & travelled immediately back. Lieut. MOSCROP rejoined adjutant in his absence	
KEMMEL SHELTERS	15th to 22nd	9 p.m.	On the night of the 15th the Battalion was relieved by the 4th YORKS REGT. and marched into Brigade reserve at KEMMEL SHELTERS. Under notice to move at 15 minutes warming. B. Coys had two additions of new fire-about this time & had given warning of the per cent of gas attack on our front and inflicted attack on the Huns, no wind was up generally likely in Brigade's reserve working parties of 150 men per night were supplied to work in the trenches in arrears hrs duty & in addn the R.E.	
Trenches G1–H1A	22/23	9 p.m.	On the night of the 22/23 the Battalion moved up to relieve G1–H1A & men and relieved the 4th Yorks. Regt.	

WAR DIARY of the 5th Durham L.I.
INTELLIGENCE SUMMARY
April, 1916

Army Form C. 2118

Place	Date	Hour	Summary of Events and Information	Remarks and references to Appendices
Toronto. G1 - H1A	April 22 to 28		The battalion was allowed one an labor 1 Coy 4th E.Yorks in support at KEMMEL CHATEAU from "A" lands to "A" land 16 & Balloon subbed A. Coy. G3R - G3L. B. Coy. G1 + G2. + 1 platoon 4th E.Yorks. C. Coy. G4 + H1A D. Coy. S.P. 10 + 11 + adjacent flats Say this by was handed up into G2S few The hours in trenches were quite than any minor one our can native amounting to 8 O.R. wounded, but owing to dampness of chlak and general "wind up" the last two in these days were trying one Lieut (att) G.O. SPENCE and unwell commands of 150th Brigade & Major H. Evans took our the Battalion This battalion was relieved by the 1st GORDON HIGHLANDERS and proceeded into Divisional Reserve at LOCRE when it alarm the night.	
LOCRE.	27th 28th	10 P.M.		
CAESTRE	29th	11.30am	The Battalion was allowed at LOCRE b/o 8th KINGS. OWN. REGT. and moved into and was at CAESTRE via BAILLEUL & METEREN. It was very hot & the men hardly cut of condition but none fell out & everyone was in fullest by 4 P.M.	
	30th		Battalion at rest in billets which were rather from fever & exceptionally good. On the night of the 29/30 the Hun. observed at reserve trench on our front with gas and at 2 A.M. the Battalion was ordered to stand to in readiness to more in case gas was used. At 5 A.M. this was countermanded & normal conditions were resumed.	

W.R. Wilson Lieut. Col. Commanding 1st Line 5th Bn. Durham L.I.

Army Form C. 2118

WAR DIARY of the 5th DURHAM L.I.
or INTELLIGENCE SUMMARY
May 1915

(Erase heading not required.)

Place	Date	Hour	Summary of Events and Information	Remarks and references to Appendices
CAESTRE	MAY 1ST		The Battalion passed into G.H.Q. Reserve and was at rest in the field around CAESTRE, which was billed in good farm billets. Whilst at rest a works programme was carried out consisting of bayonet training, Squadron covering movements, reviewing the bus, carried out and Officers & other ranks were continually attending & Army Schools & Officers of Instruction. The afternoon was devoted to football & a push down to get the men fit again. The Battalion was marched in route march, a small tactical scheme, and in attack on practise trenches. During the month we have had a draft of 50 men & 5 Officers including Capt. I. Blumer who was wounded on 26th January, 1915. Battalion attended a Divisional parade at FLETRE where the 2nd Army Commanders presented D.C.M. ribbon to Bdsm. Sergt Major THEW. Sergt Jonny & Pte Egington.	
	23d			
	24.		Battn. Kit inspection and medical inspection in the afternoon the Battn. cheerful were highly successful. 2nd Army Inspection of Battn. officers by D.M.S. at H.Q.S. and was held in field	

Army Form C. 2118

WAR DIARY of the 1/5th Durham L.I.
INTELLIGENCE SUMMARY June 1916.

(Erase heading not required.)

Instructions regarding War Diaries and Intelligence Summaries are contained in F.S. Regs., Part II. and the Staff Manual respectively. Title Pages will be prepared in manuscript.

Place	Date	Hour	Summary of Events and Information	Remarks and references to Appendices
Trenches S.1 - H.I.A. KEMMEL	12th		From June 12th to 14th the Battalion was in Brigade Reserve at Kemmel shelters & on the night of the 4/5th June it moved up to trenches & was distributed as under. A. Coy. S.P. 10 @ Fort Regina. B. " S.P.R - H.I.A. trench. C. " S.P. 11 & Fort Saskatchewan. D. " S.I. - 93. L. trench.	
	5th & 6th 13th		In trenches S.I. - H.I.A. the town was had so much enemy shell fire than normally & lot of work was put in on trenches & new shelters, lines and building a new Battn. H.Q. at Fort Saskatchewan.	
	13-14th	11 p.m.	Battalion relieved on the night of the 13/14th by the 4th Yorks & went into Divisional Reserve at Warefield Huts. Locre.	
LOCRE.	15th		In Divisional Reserve, working parties of 210 men nightly for work under R.E. & 7th D.L.I. supplied. Previous Battalion.	
	16th		Moved from Warefield Huts to York Camp, and supplied guards of 1 Officer & N.C.O's - 24 men for the Kemmel defences. When in reserve the 4th Royal Fusiliers continued to supply working parties.	
	17th	1.15 a.m.	Stand to. Divisional adjusting the Battn. to "Stand to" owing to a gas attack on the 24th Divisional front. Battn. ready to move off at 2.15 a.m. During the attack our working parties were up in the trenches - The bombardment, they manned the trenches lines - arrived in the coy bombardment. They did good work - Generally wounds & casualties. 1 killed & 3 wounded.	

Army Form C. 2118

WAR DIARY of the 5th Durham L.I.
or
INTELLIGENCE SUMMARY for May 1916.
(Erase heading not required.)

Place	Date	Hour	Summary of Events and Information	Remarks and references to Appendices
KEMMEL SHELTERS	28.	5.30 A.M.	Battalion moves from CAESTRE to KEMMEL. Transport returned to 82 Kings. Own. (R.L.) at 11.30 A.M. & harnid into Brigade reserve. Battalion left CAESTRE at 5.30 A.M. & marched via FLETRE, BAILLEUL, DRANOUTRE. Eng. was at disposal of Eng. Officer with 2nd Brigade men which partim of 250 men was so which nightly to O.C.'s Battalion in the line & 250 Eng. R.E. furnishing leg. In addition men were employed in digging chalk trenches at In Butments, wherein butt & holonging on new Brigade H.Q.'s On the night of the 31st Capt. L.L. RAIMES who had only been with in about a fortnight was wounded in the head while we unloading half at KEMMEL & died at the C.C.S. BAILLEUL the following morning.	

signature
Lieut. Col.
Commanding 1st. Line 5th. Bn. Durham L. Infy.

WAR DIARY or INTELLIGENCE SUMMARY

Army Form C. 2118

of 5th Durham L.I.

for June 1916

(Erase heading not required.)

Instructions regarding War Diaries and Intelligence Summaries are contained in F. S. Regs., Part II. and the Staff Manual respectively. Title Pages will be prepared in manuscript.

Place	Date	Hour	Summary of Events and Information	Remarks and references to Appendices
LOCRE	19th	2 pm	Moved from York camp Locre to new camping ground at N.1.A.3.1 near LA CLYTTE. This was only new ground & men were in tents & a pullout.	
Camp LA CLYTTE	20th to 30th		Whilst here the Battalion was lent to the 151st Brigade for work. Training parties of 400 men per night were sent up to work on the D.L.I. subs. along RIDGEWOOD. During the past month the following honours & awards have been given to the Regiment. Capt. H.F. WILKIN R.A.M.C. Military Cross Lieut. Col. R. GLASSPOOL Mention in Despatches Coy. Sergt. Major G.D. SPENCE " " " L/Cpl. PURVIS " " " Major H. ENSOR was promoted to substantive rank of Major.	

[signature] Lieut. Col.

Commanding 1st Line 5th. Bn. Durham L.I.

War Diary
5th Bn Durham L.I.

July 1916

Volume 16

WAR DIARY of 5th BATTN. DURHAM L.I. Army Form C. 2118
or
INTELLIGENCE SUMMARY
for JULY 1916.

(Erase heading not required.)

Instructions regarding War Diaries and Intelligence Summaries are contained in F. S. Regs., Part II. and the Staff Manual respectively. Title Pages will be prepared in manuscript.

Place	Date	Hour	Summary of Events and Information	Remarks and references to Appendices
LA. CLYTTE. Camp	July 1st		Battalion still at camp near LA. CLYTTE. where it was attached to 151st Brigade for work in the ordin., supplying 400 men per night.	
	3/4th	11 P.M.	On night of the 3/4 the Battalion relieved the 4th NORTHUMBERLAND FUSILIERS in trenches L1 to L7 disposition of Coys was as under:— A - S.P. 13 & WATSONVILLE. B - Batt. Around YORK. HOUSE. C - L1, 2, 3, 4 & L15 D - L5, 6 & 7.	
Trenches K2A to L7.	5/6		In the day, night & right Coy took over K2A & K2B trenches, which were held hitherto in turn condition & chain. Ten section of the line was the front. Bat. the Battalion had been in, in bad repair & in ambiency. One the evening of the 5th we had our first casualties owing 2 killed & 12 wounded with shell fire at S.P. 18.	
	8th		Quiet day until 6 P.M. when enemy trench mortars in frailty shelling 3 x surroundings. All night a patrol was sent out from L7 but had nothing of interest to admit; with the exception of a wandering party whilst in "L trench" with Lewis Gun.	
	12th		The situation continued normal our chief trouble still being trench mortars & m. gun running in a steady flow of casualties.	

1875 Wt. W593/826 1,000,000 4/15 J.B.C. & A. A.D.S.S /Forms/C. 2118

Army Form C. 2118

WAR DIARY of 5th DURHAM L.I. for
or
INTELLIGENCE SUMMARY JULY 1916
(Erase heading not required.)

Instructions regarding War Diaries and Intelligence Summaries are contained in F.S. Regs., Part II. and the Staff Manual respectively. Title Pages will be prepared in manuscript.

Place	Date	Hour	Summary of Events and Information	Remarks and references to Appendices
R.C. FARM.	15 &	12.	Battalion relieved by 5th YORKS. Regt. & moved into Brigade Reserve at R.C. FARM. & No.1 entrenching Battalion at N.13.D.5.2. Total casualties for last tour have been 5 killed & 37 wounded including 2 Lieut. G. DAWE who had just joined us.	
	16		While in reserve usual working parties carried out. Chinchlite training continued. Working parties of 200 men supplied nightly to the R.E.	
Tumlur G.1 to H.2	19-	11.15PM	Moved back to Tumlur G.1 - H.2 at KEMMEL relieving 4th Yorks. Regt. Distribution G.1 - G.3.1. A Coy. G.3.R. - H.2. C " B " FORT. SASKATCHEWAN - S.P.11. Reserve in KEMMEL VILLAGE, A.	
KEMMEL SHELTERS.	22/23.		Relieved by the 8th DURHAM.L.I. & marched into Divisional Reserve at KEMMEL SHELTERS. Casualties 1 killed 5 wounded.	
	23/24		On night of 23/24th we relieved the 5th YORKS in Tumlur K.2.a. to L.7 distribution as under. A Coy. K.2.a - L.15 B " L.1 - L.7. (2 Platoon in QUEBEC VILLA by day.) C " in reserve 2 Platoon YORK Ho. + 2 at SANDBAG VILLA. D " S.P.13. Relief was late than usual not being complete until 12 mid night.	

WAR DIARY of 5th DURHAM L.I.
INTELLIGENCE SUMMARY
(Erase heading not required.)

Army Form C. 2118

JULY 1916.

Place	Date	Hour	Summary of Events and Information	Remarks and references to Appendices
Trenches K2A 16 L7	July 25-27		Nothing unusual to report. The "Hun" appears to have more artillery up than during our last tour, and his rifle fire at night is more noticeable.	
	28		An exceptionally quiet day practically not a shell on our line at all. 2nd Lieut. C.R. WOOLLEY was unfortunately killed by a stray bullet whilst asleep in his bivouac at YORK. Ho.	
	30/31		Battalion relieved by 5th Yorks. Regt. & proceeded into Brigade Reserve at R.C. Farm. 2nd Lieut. C.N. SADLER was badly wounded in the late on his way out of WATLING STR. after relief. During the past few weeks a good deal of work has been done including construction of dug outs for the numerous at- YORK. Ho.	
R.C. Farm	31		Battalion rested & inspected in the afternoon a draft of 2+0 men arrived in holding party of 200 men Joined to R.E. at night.	

[signature] Lieut. Col.
Commanding 1st Line 5th. Bn. Durham L.I.

Vol. 17
No. 17

WAR DIARY of the 1/5th Durham L.I.
INTELLIGENCE SUMMARY
Aug. 1916

Army Form C. 2118

Place	Date Aug	Hour	Summary of Events and Information	Remarks and references to Appendices
KEMMEL	1st		Battalion in Brigade Reserve at R.C. Farm, worked nightly fatigue of 200 men nightly supplied to R.E. Two drafts arrived of 240 + 138 volunteers chiefly from our 2nd + 3rd line. These drafts were unfit to the B.G.C. + taken up the G.O.C. 50th Division.	
	4th		On night of 4th/5th we relieved the 5th Yorks in the L. Sundun distribution as under:— A Coy. Tunnels right of Watling Str. B " " left " " C " 2 Platoons S.P. 13 + 2 at York Ho. D " Batt. Reserve in camp near Canada Corner.	
LOCRE	7/8	11 p.m.	Battalion relieved by 9th Royal Welsh Fusiliers + marched into camp reserve at Derwant Huts LOCRE.	
CAESTRE	8th	2.30 p.m.	Marched from LOCRE to CAESTRE arriving 7 p.m. marched via MONT ROUGE, SHACHEN + FLÊTRE and were billeted in old huts two miles out CAESTRE	
AUTHEUX	11th	1 p.m.	Marched to BAILLEUL + entrained two at 1 p.m. arriving at DOULENS at 7 p.m. where we detrained. Remained there two hours resting + feeding men & at 9 p.m. marched to billeting area at AUTHEUX arriving about 1 a.m. on the 12th.	
VILLERS-BOCAGE	15th	3.30 a.m.	Marched as a Brigade from AUTHEUX to VILLERS-BOCAGE a distance of 14 miles arriving 10.30 a.m., Battalion marched by Divisional Commander thro' 1 p.m.	
MOLLIENS-AU-BOIS	16th	11.0 a.m.	Marched to MOLLIENS-AU-BOIS + bivouacked in wood, arriving thro' FIESSELES.	

Vol.
No. 17

Army Form C. 2118

Instructions regarding War Diaries and Intelligence Summaries are contained in F.S. Regs., Part II. and the Staff Manual respectively. Title Pages will be prepared in manuscript.

WAR DIARY of the 5th DURHAM. L.I.
for
INTELLIGENCE SUMMARY Aug. 1916.
(Erase heading not required.)

Place	Date Aug	Hour	Summary of Events and Information	Remarks and references to Appendices
KEMMEL.	1st		Battalion in Brigade Reserve at R.C. FARM, worked on trenches & keeping carried out - working parties of 200 men nightly supplied to R.E. Two drafts arrived of 240 & 138 respectively. Staffing from one 2nd & 3rd line. Three drafts were inspected by the D.G.C. & taken up the G.O.C. 50th Division.	
	4th		On night of 4th/5th we relieved the 5th YORKS. in the L. Trenches, distribution as under:— A Coy Trenches right of WATLING STR. B " " left " " " " C " 2 Platoon S.P. 13 & 2 at YORK Ho. D " Batt. Reserve in camp near CANADA CORNER.	
LOCRE.	7/8	11 p.m.	Battalion relieved by 9th ROYAL WELSH FUSILIERS & marched into camp numbers at DONAULI Hut LOCRE.	
CAESTRE	8th	2.30 p.m.	Marched from LOCRE to CAESTRE arriving 7 p.m. marched by MONT. ROUGE, SHECHEN & FLETRE, and reached our old billets there.	
	9th		At and at CAESTRE.	
AUTHEUX.	11th	1 p.m.	Marched to BAILLEUL & entrained there at 1 p.m. arriving at DOULENS at 7 p.m. where we detrained. Remained there two hours resting & feeding men & at 9 p.m. march to billeting area at AUTHEUX arriving about 1 a.m. on the 12th.	
VILLERS BOCAGE	15th	3.30 a.m.	Marched as a Brigade from AUTHEUX to VILLERS-BOCAGE a distance of 14 miles. arriving 10.30 a.m., Battalion reached the Divnl Commanders truce in wood near FLESSELLES.	
MOLLIENS-Au-Bois.	16th	11.0 a.m.	Marched to MOLLIENS-AU-BOIS & Bivouacked arriving there at 1 p.m.	

Vol. 17.
2/

Army Form C. 2118

WAR DIARY of 5th DURHAM. L.I.
or INTELLIGENCE SUMMARY Aug. 1516.
(Erase heading not required.)

Instructions regarding War Diaries and Intelligence Summaries are contained in F.S. Regs., Part II. and the Staff Manual respectively. Title Pages will be prepared in manuscript.

Place	Date	Hour	Summary of Events and Information	Remarks and references to Appendices
MORIENS.	17th	5 AM	Paraded Baiseux & Hennencourt	
MILLENCOURT	18.		Communal Training & musketry, doing 5 hours daily	
	21.		All Officers lectured by the B.G.C.	
	24.		Brigade Scheme in afternoon, attack upon the skeen	
	25th		Batt. H.Q. hostered in Div. contest hotel with No. 4 squad. R.F.C. around Baiseux attendance on completion.	
	27th		Brigade Tactical Scheme attack on hunden	
	28th		Brigade Ceremonial Parade. Inspection by Corps. Commander in hutin, camillis around to walton.	
	29.		Coys + Battalion Training continued	
	30.			
	31.		Brigade Scheme attack on hunden — contact patrol work practised.	

[signature]
Lieut. Col.
Commanding 5th Durham. L.I.

Vol. 17.

Army Form C. 2118

WAR DIARY of 5th DURHAM L.I.
or
INTELLIGENCE SUMMARY Aug. 1916.
(Erase heading not required.)

Instructions regarding War Diaries and Intelligence Summaries are contained in F.S. Regs., Part II. and the Staff Manual respectively. Title Pages will be prepared in manuscript.

Place	Date	Hour	Summary of Events and Information	Remarks and references to Appendices
MOLLIENS	17th	5 A.M.	Paraded for BAISEUX & HENNENCOURT where the Battalion was billeted	
MILLENCOURT	18th		Commenced Training & musketry, doing 5 hour daily	
	21st		All Officers entered by the B.G.C.	
	24th		Brigade Schemes in afternoon, attack over the open	
	25th		Batt. H.Q. practised in Div. contest hotel with all No. 4 squad. R.F.C. around, attending conference on completion	
			BAISEUX	
	27th		Brigade Tactical Scheme, attack on trenches	
	28th		Brigade Ceremonial Parade, preparatory to Corps Commander in review, cancelled owing to wet weather	
	29th		Coy & Battalion Training continued	
	30th			
	31st		Brigade Scheme, attack on trenches + bombed hostile with material	

[signature] Lieut. Col.
Commanding 5th Durham L.I.

150th. INFANTRY BRIGADE
50th. DIVISION

5th. DURHAM LIGHT INFANTRY

150th. INFANTRY BRIGADE

SEPTEMBER 1916.

150th. INFANTRY BRIGADE
50th. DIVISION

WAR DIARY of 5TH DURHAM. L.I.

INTELLIGENCE SUMMARY
SEPTEMBER 1916.
VOL 15

Army Form C. 2118

Place	Date	Hour	Summary of Events and Information	Remarks and references to Appendices
MILLENCOURT	1		Battalion continued carrying out Coy & Batt. training.	
	2		Inspection by B.G.C. 150. Brigade	
	3		Brigade Church Parade in field near Henencourt	
	4		Divisional field day near HENENCOURT. Brigade practiced attack on Kunber 3rd D.L.I. in advance.	
	9	4.30 p.m	Battalion marched to BECOURT WOOD, via ALBERT, arriving at 7-0 p.m. and after much reading about for tea settled down in the woods near BECOURT - LA BOISELLE road at 9.30 p.m.	
	10		At BECOURT Wood. Officer reconnoitred trenches - working parties were supplied by day & night on numerous jobs preparatory to beginning offensive.	
	11		Capt. H.A. WILSON killed in the ENE. trench while in charge of a Battalion working party. His body was recovered after much difficulty & was buried at BECOURT military cemetery the following morning.	
	14	7.30 p.m	Battalion about 650 rifles strong went up to take part in offensive operations & marched via CONTALMAISON & MAMETZ Wood to BEZANTIN- LE- PETIT where an assembly in the old german line with A - B in O.C.L. C - D + H.Q.'s in O.G.1. was accomplished by 6.20 a.m. the following morning which was the time fixed on 2 hours before	

Page 2.

of 5th DURHAM L.I.

WAR DIARY
or
INTELLIGENCE SUMMARY
(Erase heading not required.)

for September 1916   Vol. 18

Army Form C. 2118

Place	Date	Hour	Summary of Events and Information	Remarks and references to Appendices
BEZANTIN - LE - PETIT	15	6.30 A.M.	At this hour the bombardment commenced & the assault took place. This Bn. arranging this was followed up by A Coy under Capt. HILL & the remnant of B Coy under Lieut. J.K.M. HESSLER. C Coy under Lieut. F.D. BROWN went forward to the Bde of objective. D Coy in reg'tal reserve under Capt. P. WOOD moved up into Batt'n H.Q. at 7.20 a.m. into SWANSEA trench.	
	16	9.0 A.M.	5th D.L.I. attacked by Coy of 4th E. YORKS were ordered to attack & hold STARFISH & PRUE trenches. This Coy was reinforced all own ranks with great difficulty the attack was launched in turn D, B, C. A log in reserve [?] at the beginning but afterwards the D Coy and also this war lorn end of STARFISH – PRUE trenches were addressed. A good proportion of casualties was suffered from m.g. fire & from a com. trans. no action taking information could be obtained of the situation but by 12 noon on the 17th it was decided that enemies still held most of PRUE & hook of the CRESCENT & hold was hurled up STARFISH but was however held. At 5.30 p.m. a bombing attack was again set up in an attempt by bombing parties of 4th & 5th YORKS. This attack was fulfilling its aims Lieut. E. GREVILLE - JONES & both objectives were taken & Bde again in normal counter attacks. Division of Batt. was then than B & D Coys in PRUE A & C STARFISH. Batt. H.Q. MARTIN TRENCH.	
	18		8 loud feet & garrison much thing trenches fairly heavy & taken casualties	

Army Form C. 2118

Page 8
WAR DIARY of 5th DURHAM. L.I.
or
INTELLIGENCE SUMMARY for September 1916.
(Erase heading not required.)   Vol. 13.

Instructions regarding War Diaries and Intelligence Summaries are contained in F. S. Regs., Part II. and the Staff Manual respectively. Title Pages will be prepared in manuscript.

Place	Date	Hour	Summary of Events and Information	Remarks and references to Appendices
	19.		At 10.A.M. we were relieved by 5th Yorks. who got lost on the way & did not reach H.Qrs much delayed.	
	20.		Out out in O.C.I. arrangements for a Battn. working party was submitted to O.C. 7 Field Coy. R.E. for work on roads near MAMETZ WOOD	
	22.			
	23.	7.45 P.M.	March up to trenches when we relieved units of 145. Brigade in STARFISH & TRUE trenches up to the CRESCENT.	
	24.		Holding lines & advanced posts. Enemy was a quiet day until about 7.30 P.M. when H.Qs. in a sunken road was shelled, several direct hits being made on it.	
	25.		Attack by 12th Division on our right. H.Qs. was again shelled. 6th D.L.I. came up to dig our assembly trench about 800 yds. in front of trench running from MARTINPUICH. Much trouble caused through no guides being available & 6th D.L.I. did not no digging tils wandered about until 3 A.M.	
	26.	12°	Relieved by 5th YORKS & went into CLARKS & HOOK trenches when we stayed until 5 P.M. then moved up to Hamlin again for the one attack on the 26th & 5th Yorks line at 11.0 P.M. signal a dump was met German line was to attack even them at 4th & 5th YORKS.	

1875   Wt. W593/826   1,000,000   4/15   J.B.C. & A.   A.D.S.S./Forms/C.2118.

Page 4

WAR DIARY of 5th DURHAM. L.I
for September 1916.
INTELLIGENCE SUMMARY
Vol. 18.

(Erase heading not required.)

Army Form C. 2118

Place	Date	Hour	Summary of Events and Information	Remarks and references to Appendices
	26.	11.P.M	suffered on right flank by 4th E. YORKS and on left by ... CRESCENT ALLEY and an enfiladed MACHINE GUN near MARTINPUICH. We were to advance up CRESCENT ALLEY. After an Bombing party + 1 Lewis gun under Lieut H. GREEN. Our division was A.C. & D. Coys with B. Coy in reserve. At the start the advance was muddled, partly owing to troops being unable to find the taped out assembly trench, & partly to 5th YORKS forming division & getting into CRESCENT ALLEY thinking it was their objective, then blocking our frontier & by when was unloading up the ALLEY.	
	27.	12 noon	5th D.L.I. launched a battle patrol up CRESCENT ALLEY to objective. This worked onwards and the whole objective was gained by 1.P.M.	
			At 7.P.M. we were ordered to extend our left flank through 23 Division in an left + push outwards through FLERS LINE as hated under head on GREEN line due. So "D" Coy was hurried up to occupy + enough but it was found trench remains held, as a trench had to be established in C.T.	

EAUCOURT. L'ABBAYE
1ST DIVISION
23 DIVISION
FLERS LINE
LE. SARS.
D Coy S.P.
C. Coy S.P.
CRESCENT ALLEY
ASSEMBLY LINE
MARTINPUICH

WAR DIARY or INTELLIGENCE SUMMARY

Army Form C. 2118

Page 5
5th Durham L.I.
September 1916. Vol. 18

Place	Date	Hour	Summary of Events and Information	Remarks and references to Appendices
O.G.I. BAZENTIN LE PETIT	28.	8 AM.	Battalion in relieved by 8th D.L.I. + harned into D minimal running in	
	29.		J.m. D minimal Reserves, moved at 5 p.m. into our own MAMETZ WOOD.	
MAMETZ WOOD	30.		In MAMETZ WOOD. morquining + hutwning for trentus.	

(signature) Lieut. Col.
Commanding 1st. Line 5th. Bn. Durham L.I.

WAR DIARY
or
INTELLIGENCE SUMMARY

(Erase heading not required.)

Army Form C. 2118

Vol 13

6th Battalion
The Durham Light Infantry
October 1916
Vol. XIX

WAR DIARY or INTELLIGENCE SUMMARY

Army Form C. 2118

Place	Date	Hour	Summary of Events and Information	Remarks and references to Appendices
MAMETZ WOOD	1st Oct		Moved from MAMETZ WOOD to O.G.1 where we were in Divisional reserve. Battn had to be in position at 1 P.M. and reached their lines until 3.15 P.M. likely were 2 hrs late. Had an attack in the FLERS LINES. At which time 3 Coys were in BOTTOM WOOD. Remained in the trenches to carry hot supplies & food to troops & duties in O.G.1.	
O.G.1	2nd Oct		300 men supplied at 8 A.M. for same work as previous day. Battn moved back to MAMETZ WOOD & remained there the day which was very wet.	
MAMETZ WOOD	3rd Oct	9. A.M.	Batt. MAMETZ moved via LOZENGE WOOD to ALBERT where we billeted in some old huts who were vacated by our Cavalry.	
ALBERT	4th Oct	8.30 A.M.	Batt. ALBERT & moved via MILLENCOURT & HENENCOURT to BAIZIEUX WOOD where we went into camp.	
BAIZIEUX WOOD	5th 6th 12th		At BAIZIEUX WOOD. Coys carried out Company training & the training of specialists was continued.	
BAIZIEUX WD	13th		Battn carried out Relieve and Brigade Scheme at 8 P.M. practising assembling and taken by night to an attack.	
BAIZIEUX WOOD	14th 15th 22nd		Company training & specialists work continued. Two Brigade field days. Practising assembling & advancing to the attack & night on a Company training. Outpost scheme near MONTIGNY. Transport Inspection by GOC Division.	
BAIZIEUX WD	22nd			
BAIZIEUX WOOD	23rd	11 A.M.	C.O. & O.C. Companies visited trenches from BAIZIEUX WOOD to MILLENCOURT where we billeted.	
MILLENCOURT	24th	2 P.M.	Moved from MILLENCOURT via ALBERT, BECOURT & CONTALMAISON to MAMETZ WOOD but on arrival were led an ill. BAZENTIN-LE-GRAND. Old roads were bad & the transport was heavy. Battn had being billeted in tents till 12 midnight.	
BAZENTIN	25th		at BAZENTIN.	
	26th 27th		Working parties of 175 supplied to R.E. in front line & shelters. Working parties again supplied to R.E. for work on the PRUE & STARFISH lines.	

Army Form C. 2118

WAR DIARY
or
INTELLIGENCE SUMMARY
(Erase heading not required.)

Instructions regarding War Diaries and Intelligence Summaries are contained in F.S. Regs., Part II. and the Staff Manual respectively. Title Pages will be prepared in manuscript.

Place	Date	Hour	Summary of Events and Information	Remarks and references to Appendices
BAZENTIN LE GRAND	28th		Moved up to trenches & took over from the 5th YORKSHIRE REGT. Dispositions as follows: B coy in the SNAG - THE trenches, A coy in ABBAYE LANE, C & D coys in support.	
à Trenches	27th		The FLERS SWITCH. A quiet day but very wet. Casualties & wounded.	
	30th		Another quiet day but still very wet. At night A coy. moved up from close support & relieved B coy in the SNAG - THIS trench. B coy came back to close support in ABBAYE LANE.	
	31st		Again wet. C & D coys spent working parties in the trenches & front of SNAG trench & to FLERS LINE. During the month the following have been awarded the Military medal, as follows:- 2/Lt LUKE, Sergt O'DELL, Cpl HANSELL, L/Cpl HARPER, Pte Chas Smith, Pte DENNY. We also have received a draft of recruits - 7 Officers.	

W Lewis Lt
OC 5 Durham coy

Volume 20. 5th Batt. DURHAM. L.I.

Secret

Army Form C. 2118.

WAR DIARY
or
INTELLIGENCE SUMMARY
(Erase heading not required.)

November 1916

Vol 17

Place	Date	Hour	Summary of Events and Information	Remarks and references to Appendices
FLERS LINE TRENCHES	1/11/16 to 2/11/16		Relieved by 5' Yorkshire Regt. A + B Coys to FLERS LINE, C + D Coys to TRUE TRENCH. Batt. H.Qrs. to FLERS LINE. All in trench for relief.	
Bazentin le Grand	3/11/16		Battalion proceeded to Bazentin le Grand.	
Mametz	3/11/16		Moved to Camp S. of Mametz Wood. Working parties supplied to R.E. for work on Light Railway.	
"	4/11/16		Working parties to R.E. day & night. Military Medals awarded to:— 695 Cpl. Pte. Allen J. 312 " " Dickson J.C. Sgt. 9 " Sgt. Jackson B. 290 L/Cpl. Burns W. 1706 L/Cpl. Daniell F. (Bar)	1605 Pte. Garton W. 232-9 " Yates J. (Bar) 1477 " Mahin 2195 Sgt. M'Carthy 211 L/Cpl. Curris J. 2513 " Hyde L.T. E.L. 131 Pte. ... L... attack
"	5/11/16		Battalion under 10 minutes notice all ready to move on Butte de Warlencourt.	
Bivouacs E. of Mametz	6/11/16		Relieved the C + D Coys ... ... the a.m. C + D Coys on the ... ... Mametz trenches Ridge in the ...	83/-

1875 Wt. W593/826 1,000,000 4/15 J.B.C. & A. A.D.S.S./Forms/C.2118.

Army Form C. 2118

WAR DIARY
or
INTELLIGENCE SUMMARY

(Erase heading not required.)

2 Cmla

Place	Date	Hour	Summary of Events and Information	Remarks and references to Appendices
Trenches	6/7/16		In the trenches. 10 Coy in Albere Trench.	
"	7/7/16		Inter company relief.	
"	8/7/16		Inter company relief.	
"	9/7/16		Battalion relieved by the 5/Dorset Yorkshire Regt. A B & D Coys to Fleurs Switch. C Coy to Flers Line.	
"	10/7/16		Working parts to dig new trench near Marsh Road. Very experienced use of the heavier though since our arrival on the SOMME.	
"	11/7/16		Battalion relieved by 1/Battalion 1/0 Northumberland Fusiliers and moved back to BAZENTIN le GRAND. 10 casualties received. Battalion under 10 minutes notice to reinforce the 1/9 Infantry Bde in attack on the High Wood Line.	8·30

Army Form C. 2118

WAR DIARY
or
INTELLIGENCE SUMMARY

(Erase heading not required.)

Instructions regarding War Diaries and Intelligence Summaries are contained in F.S. Regs., Part II. and the Staff Manual respectively. Title Pages will be prepared in manuscript.

Place	Date	Hour	Summary of Events and Information	Remarks and references to Appendices
Buzancy to Bazoux	16/11/16		Battalion relieved by the 10th Bat Yorks Regiment and much track to Beauval.	
Beauval	17/11/16 to 29/11/16		Battalion supplied large working parties daily to work on the Rippe roads.	
Bazoux	30/11/16		Battalion moved further back to camp for Bazoux for one months training.	

Hugh Jeffreys, Lieut. Col.
Commanding 1st. Line 5th. Bn. Durham L.I.

Volume 20

5th BATTALION DURHAM LIGHT INFANTRY WAR DIARY

VOLUME IV FOR DECEMBER 1916

INTELLIGENCE SUMMARY

Army Form C. 2118

1/5 DLI

Place	Date	Hour	Summary of Events and Information	Remarks and references to Appendices
Bayeux	Dec.1		Training Battalion Parade.	
	2		Training Battalion Parade	
	3		Church Parade on Battn. Parade ground	
	4		Companies at disposal of O.C. Coys for Coy training. Specialists under Specialist Officers	
	5		Inspection of new draft by C.O. Company training. Specialists under Specialist Officers	
	6		Company training. Inspection of new draft by C.O. Battalion allotted the Baths in Bayeux all day.	
	7		Company training. Range allotted to B & C Coys.	
	8		Company training. Range allotted to A & D Coys.	
	9		Company training continued. Range allotted to Lewis Gunners & A. Company.	
	10		Church Parade on Battn. Parade ground.	
	11		Company & Specialist training continued. Inspection of draft by C.O. Range allotted to Lewis Gunners.	
	12		Company & Specialist training continued. Range allotted to Lewis Gunners & A. Coy.	

WAR DIARY or INTELLIGENCE SUMMARY

Army Form C. 2118

Place	Date	Hour	Summary of Events and Information	Remarks and references to Appendices
	Dec 13		Company Training continued. Tactical attack scheme for all Officers under Commanding Officer	
	14		Brigade Range allotted to the Battalion.	
	15		Company training continued. Specialists under Specialist Officers	
	16		Ditto	
	17		Church Parade.	
	18		Battalion allotted Baths in Bavaux	
	19		Practice attack on Trenches by Coys starting with A Coy. Inspection by Brigadier G.C.	
	20		Battalion Tactical exercise for all Officers & N.C.Os. Company Training continued	
	21		Contact Patrol scheme for selected Officers & N.C.Os. Company training continued.	
	22		Inspection of Transport by Brigadier. Brigadier G.C. Night scheme under Brigade arrangements. Final of inter-platoon football competition – 5' Platoon winners. Lecture by C.R.A. for selected Officers at Pontay.	

WAR DIARY
or
INTELLIGENCE SUMMARY

(Erase heading not required.)

Army Form C. 2118

Place	Date	Hour	Summary of Events and Information	Remarks and references to Appendices
	Dec 23		Brigade Sports. Concert at Night.	
	24		Company Training. Tactical Scheme for Officers & N.C.Os. Range allotted to Lewis Gunners.	
	25		Church Parade. Brigade Paper Chase.	
	26		Company Training. Brigade exercises for selected Officers & N.C.Os.	
	27		Contact Patrol Scheme for Officers. Company Training continued.	
	28		Battalion Parade for Battalion Drill	
	29		Company Training continued. Brigade Range allotted to Battalion	
	30		Battalion moved up to Billets at Albert.	
Albert	31		Company Training	

Lieut. Col.
Commanding 1st Lincs 6th. Bn. Durham L. Infty.

VOLUME 21

Vol. 22.   5 BN. DURHAM LIGHT INFANTRY WAR DIARY   JANUARY 1917

Army Form C. 2118

INTELLIGENCE SUMMARY
(Erase heading not required.)

15/10

Vol 19

59+
13

Place	Date	Hour	Summary of Events and Information	Remarks and references to Appendices
Albert	Jan 1.		Moved from Albert to Morgenchi to Port.	
			The following awards were announced in the Birthday Honours list:	
			Lieut. Col. G. O. Spence — D.S.O.	DESTINATION
			Major William Roch Mocarta — M.C.	D.S.O.
			Lieut Eric Gurthe Jones — M.C.	M C
			Lsgt C. A. Neill — M.D.	M D
			L/cpl Green — M.D.	M D
Morgenchi Albert	4/1		The Battalion relieved the 6th N.F. in trenches in front of Leeds Trench with A & D Coys in the line, C Coy in support & B in reserve at DETHIC'S Camp near Morey Abbaye.	
Front line near Morey Abbaye	9/10		To Bienfaine and a Company intrenched. C Coy proceeded to Eawcourt village.	
	11/2		Battalion relieved by 1 Yorks Regt approached to Havre Suppose. During relief a heavy barrage was placed by the enemy on Lechin Comp. Estimates on our Battalion we had 1 Casualty	

Army Form C. 2118

WAR DIARY
or
INTELLIGENCE SUMMARY
(Erase heading not required.)

Instructions regarding War Diaries and Intelligence Summaries are contained in F.S. Regs., Part II. and the Staff Manual respectively. Title Pages will be prepared in manuscript.

Place	Date	Hour	Summary of Events and Information	Remarks and references to Appendices
Thimbles	15/16 Jan.		Battalion relieved by 6 N.F. and proceeded to 113 Brigade Reserve Pott.	
Bayencke Pott.	23/27		Battalion relieved the 6 N.F. in trenches on Grand Flohaux Front with one Coy in the line, C Company at Toncourt, 2 Platoons Coy in reserve at Details Camp. A very quiet tour	
—	27/28		Battalion relieved by the 2nd Australian Battalion & proceeded to Bayencke Pott. 6 Plat. Puts.	
Vaucourt	28		Battalion proceeded to camp at "Trevor Park"	
Beun	30		Battalion left Trevor Park & proceeded to Beun	
"	31		Coys at disposal of Co Commanders for inspection etc	

R. J. Hunn Lt Col
for O. a. Durham L.I.
Cmdg 5 Batt Durham L.I.

5 Batt
DURHAM
LIGHT
INFANTRY

VOLUME
22

JANUARY
1917

Confidential

Headquarters
150th Infantry Bde.

Attached is War Diary
for month of February 1917.

[signature]
Lieut. Col.
Commanding 1st. Line 5th. Bn. Durham L. Infty.

WAR DIARY
or
INTELLIGENCE SUMMARY

Army Form C. 2118

(Erase heading not required.)

Commanding 1st Line 5th Bn. Durham L. Infty.
Lieut. Col.
[signature]

Place	Date	Hour	Summary of Events and Information	Remarks and references to Appendices
BUIRE	1/2/17		Companies at disposal O.C. Coys. for Platoon training. Inspection of Draft leave Jan 19th 1917 by B.G.C.	
do	2/2/17		Brigade Route March. Route S.2.3.b.4.1. - Cross Roads D.6.C. - Road Junction C27.b - Flaucourt - Barleux - Cross Roads D5.b.6. - Biaches - Road Junction Villers - Bretonneux ?	
do	3/1/17 to 5/2/17		Divine Service. Coys at disposal of O.C. Coys for Platoon training ? Rifle Range allotted to Companies. Training of Specialists under Specialist Officers (continued) Bombing tct under Bergd. arrangements of 2 fields near for platoon	
MORCOURT	9.2.17		Battalion moved from BUIRE to MORCOURT Route - VILLE - MORLANCOURT - CHIPILLY - CERISY - MORCOURT. Paraded at 9.30 a.m full marching order 100% between Companies	
	10.2.17		Battalion moved from MORCOURT to FOUCAUCOURT. Route - City Road S.23.A93 Cross Roads R 27.C.9.2 Parade 10 am in full marching order 100% between Companies	
FOUCAUCOURT	11.2.17 to 12.2.17		Coys at disposal of O.C. Coys. Inspection of Draft by C.O. Coys at disposal of O.C. Coys - looking parties to work on Rachery Trench.	
,,	13.2.17 to 19/2/17		Coys at Kilo Road A.C.C. Coys. Working Parties to work on trenches in new Sec Fr.	

WAR DIARY
INTELLIGENCE SUMMARY

6TH BN DURHAM LIGHT INFANTRY

VOLUME 23

FEBRUARY

SECRET

5 Bn DURHAM LIGHT INFANTRY
FEBRUARY 1917.
VOLUME N°. 23.

Army Form C. 2118

WAR DIARY
or
INTELLIGENCE SUMMARY
(Erase heading not required.)

1/5 DLI   Vol 20

Place	Date	Hour	Summary of Events and Information	Remarks and references to Appendices
FOUCACOURT	15.2.16 / 16.2.16	Night	Battalion relieved 4th Bn. YORKSHIRE REGT. in trenches. Distribution as follows: A. C & B Coys in front line D Coy in support	
La Truchée	16.2.17 to 20.2.17		In trenches	
FOUCACOURT	20.2.17		Relieved in trenches by 8th Bn. Durham L.I. - east moved back to billets in FOUCACOURT	
do	21.2.17		Coys at disposal of O.C. Coys.	
do	22.2.17 to 24.2.17		Coys at disposal of O.C. Coys - 300 men billeted - washing baths around & Coys	
do	25.2.17		Coys at disposal of O.C. Coys - Platoon spectators training	
do	26.2.17		Divine Service a/noon - inspection of Battalion by G.O.C. 50th Divn.	
do	27.2.17		Coys at disposal of O.C. Coys. Pulling up for trenches. Working parties for R.E.	
do	28.2.17		Battalion relieved 7th Bn. N.F. in reserve dugout at BELLOY-EN-SANTERRE. night of 28/1/17. A. Coy in Close support to Bn. in the line. B.C.+D Coys in dugouts in BELLOY. Paraded at 5 p.m. Moved off 5.30 p.m. "on 30 between Platoons	

Volume 24 for March 1917 • 5th Bn DURHAM • LIGHT INFANTRY

Army Form C. 2118

WAR DIARY or INTELLIGENCE SUMMARY

Vol 71

Place	Date	Hour	Summary of Events and Information	Remarks and references to Appendices
Belloy	1st – 3rd		Battalion in Belloy Support Line in support to 4th Yorks. 200 men supplied nightly for wiring the reserve line	
	3rd/4th		Battalion moved up to Trenches and relieved the 4th Yorks in the Left Sub sector – Headquarters at P.C. Gravey. The P.O. Adjt. 9.O. & B.O. and 1 officer per coy from the 2nd & 5th Lincolns joined the Battalion to be attached for instruction. Disposition of Batt in trenches – (A & D) in front line (B) in support – (C) in reserve	
	4th/5th		On the nights of 4th/5th one platoon from both B & A coys were relieved by platoons from 2nd & 5th Lincolns. A relieves C, B relieves D	
	5th/6th		Inter coy reliefs (C & D) each have platoons relieved by platoons of 2/5th Lincolns	

Army Form C. 2118

WAR DIARY
or
INTELLIGENCE SUMMARY
(Erase heading not required.)

Instructions regarding War Diaries and Intelligence Summaries are contained in F. S. Regs., Part II. and the Staff Manual respectively. Title Pages will be prepared in manuscript.

Place	Date	Hour	Summary of Events and Information	Remarks and references to Appendices
	7th/8th	a.m.	Battalion relieved in Trenches by 2/5th Lincolns & goes back into Bgde reserve in Triangle Wood	
	8th	a.m.	Batt relieved at Triangle Wood by 2/5th Leicesters & moved to Camp 59	
	9th	a.m.	Bayonetteers marching off at 2 p.m.	
	10th	a.m.	Batt at Bayonetteers. Pays at disposal of O.C. Pays for cleaning up	
	11th	a.m.	Pays at disposal of O.C. Pays	
	12th	a.m.	Church Parade	
	13th	a.m.	Pays at disposal of O.C. Pays — Batt fitted with Small Box Respirators	
	14th	a.m.	Programme of Platoon Training carried out. Baths at Morcourt	
	15th	a.m.	Training continued. Baths at Morcourt	
	16th	a.m.	Training continued	
	17th	a.m.	Training continued	
	18th	a.m.	Church Parade	
	19th	a.m.	Training continued	
	20th	a.m.		

WAR DIARY
or
INTELLIGENCE SUMMARY

(Erase heading not required.)

Army Form C. 2118

Place	Date	Hour	Summary of Events and Information	Remarks and references to Appendices
	21st		A & B Coys isolated owing to Scarlet Fever	
	22nd		Training continued. Inter Platoon competition begun	
	23rd		Training continued. Battle of Movement	
	24th		B & D Coys Tactical exercise	
	25th		Church Parade.	
	26th		Platoon competition completed. Training continued	
	27th		Training continued	
	28th		Brigade Inspection by 3rd Corps Commander. Brigade was photographed	
	29th		Isolation of A & B Coys ended. Training continued.	
	30th		Battalion moved to Grenville	
	31st		Battalion moved from La Neuville to Picquigny	

Lieut. Col.
Commanding 1st. Line 5th. Bn. Durham L. Infty.

5th Bn. Durham L. Infantry

VOLUME 94
MARCH 1917

INTELLIGENCE SUMMARY
or
WAR DIARY

5th BN DURHAM LIGHT INFANTRY APRIL 1917.
VOLUME 25 for month APRIL 1917.

Vol XXV

Place	Date	Hour	Summary of Events and Information	Remarks and references to Appendices
PIERREGOT	1st April		Batt Church Parade. Tactical Scheme for Offs carried out in the afternoon	
"	2nd "		Batt moved from PIERREGOT at midday proceeded to TALMAS	
TALMAS	3rd "		Batt moved from TALMAS at 9.0am marched to GEZAINCOURT	
GEZAINCOURT	4th "		Batt moved from GEZAINCOURT marched to BONNIERES	
BONNIERES	5th "		Coys Practical in trench digging	
"	6th "		Coys at disposal of O.C. Coys.	
"	7th "		Batt moved from BONNIERES at 9.0am marched to BERLENCOURT	
BERLENCOURT	8th "		Batt moved from BERLENCOURT at 10.15 pm marched to LIENCOURT	
LIENCOURT	9th "		Batt training under C.O.	
"	10th "		Batt moved from LIENCOURT at 2.30am marched to NOYELLETTE	
NOYELLETTE	11th "		Batt at NOYELLETTE under short notice to move	
"	12th "		Batt started from NOYELLETTE at 6.0am marched to ARRAS. Batt billeted in Caves at the FAUBOURG RONVILLE.	
ARRAS	13th "		Batt supplied working parties for work in tunnels	
"	14th "		Supplied working & Carrying parties.	
"	15th "		The 150th Bde relieved 151 Bde. The 5th Durham L.I. remained in reserve in the Caves. Otherk Bn. going into action remained behind with Major H. Eden attached at No 34 Rue St Jean ARRAS.	
"	16-17th		In reserve in the Caves	

WAR DIARY or INTELLIGENCE SUMMARY

Army Form C. 2118

Place	Date	Hour	Summary of Events and Information	Remarks and references to Appendices
	19th		Batt relieved the 7th NORTHUMBERLAND FUSILIERS in NIGER TRENCH near WANCOURT. Batt moved off at 1PM & marches via BEURAINS & TELEGRAPH HILL. Coys were shelled on the way up & suffered a few casualties.	
	20th		The Batt was relieved in NIGER TRENCH by the 4th YORKS & moved up to the trench line by WANCOURT TOWER & until we from the 4th & 5th NORTHUMBERLAND FUSILIERS. From midnight until 8am we were shelled continually by our own heavies & caused casualties & several casualties were caused.	
	21st		On the night of 21st/22nd the Batt was relieved in the front line by the 4th EAST YORKS & 4th YORKS & moved back to NIGER TRENCH.	
	22nd		In NIGER TRENCH. Batt supplied working & carrying parties & prepared for going into the attack on the following day. Moved from NIGER trench to C and right early of the river at WANCOURT in support to the left Battn - 4th YORKS at Zero — D coy sent to reinforce the left flank of 4th YORKS. An hour later B coy moved up to support the left at the Hendecourt Road. Heavy casualties.	
	23rd		11.30am the enemy counterattacked at centre & left flank. The Batt took up positions in front his trench. The Batt was in support to the 9th Durham L.I. in an enemy attack. Went as far as the SUNKEN ROAD. The Batt was relieved at night by the 8th Durham L.I. Thereon back to the trench East of the HAPP.	

Army Form C. 2118

WAR DIARY
or
INTELLIGENCE SUMMARY
(Erase heading not required.)

Instructions regarding War Diaries and Intelligence Summaries are contained in F.S. Regs., Part II. and the Staff Manual respectively. Title Pages will be prepared in manuscript.

Place	Date	Hour	Summary of Events and Information	Remarks and references to Appendices
	25th April		Moved from bivouac HARP to billets at ARRAS after being relieved by the 9th R.B.	
	26th		Billets allotted to Coys in ARRAS. Batt. entrained at ARRAS Station for MONDICOURT. Marched from MONDICOURT to HALLOY.	
HALLOY	27th		Billets at HALLOY. Coys at disposal of O.C. Coys for reorganising & equipping.	
"	28th		Coys at disposal of O.C. Coys. Baptist at 11 am. Brigadier General Price congrats bath on their recent fighting.	
"	29th		Church Parade.	
"	30th		Coys at disposal of O.C. Coys.	
			Casualties for operations of April 28th	

Killed	Wounded	Missing
Officers 4	Officers 3	Officers 1
O.R. 23	O.R. 137	O.R. 96
TOTAL Officers 8		256 Other Ranks

Capt W. MARLEY
2/Lt F.W. HEAP } Killed
2/Lt A.R. HERRING

2/Lt PEREIRA missing
2/Lt C.D. MARLEY Wounded
2/Lt R.J. STOCKDALE "
2/Lt E.W. WEEKS Shell Shock

Lieut. E.W. COULSON MAYNE Adjutant

[Signature]
Lieut. Col.
Commanding 1st. Line 5th. Bn, Durham L. Infty.

WAR DIARY
INTELLIGENCE SUMMARY

5 Bn Durham Light Infantry
VOLUME 25
For Month of
APRIL
1917

5th DURHAM LIGHT INFANTRY

WAR DIARY or INTELLIGENCE SUMMARY

Army Form C. 2118.

VOLUME 26 for MAY. 1917

Vol 23

Place	Date	Hour	Summary of Events and Information	Remarks and references to Appendices
HALLOY	MAY 1st		Battalion warned to move up to front area again left Halloy at 4.0 P.M. and marched to Chestnut Camp (COIGNEUX) about 10 miles	
COIGNEUX	2nd		Left at 3.30 P.M. & marched to FICHEUX about 12 miles hot & dusty march went into tents at Ficheux & were under short notice to move	
FICHEUX	3rd		at FICHEUX.	
	4th		Received orders at 3.0 P.M. to move at 4.0 P.M. to COIGNEUX a very hot & dusty march in which several men dropped out. Arrived COIGNEUX at	
COIGNEUX	5th	9.0 P.M.	Left COIGNEUX at 4.30 P.M. & marched via THIEVRES to HALLOY where we occupied our old billets	
HALLOY	6th		Church Parade.	
	7th		Coy Training under Coy arrangements Officers Classes	
	8th		Batt. Training cancelled owing to weather	
	9th		Specialist Training Range practice Batt took part in Brigade night operation scheme laying out Tapes Trenches – assembling – Returned to billets 1.0 a.m.	
	10th		Marching on Somme & digging	
	11th		Batt Training.	
	12		Specialist Training – Range practice – Coys at disposal of O.C. Coys. Batt took part in Brigade field firing.	

Army Form C. 2118.

WAR DIARY
or
INTELLIGENCE SUMMARY.
(Erase heading not required.)

Instructions regarding War Diaries and Intelligence Summaries are contained in F. S. Regs., Part II. and the Staff Manual respectively. Title pages will be prepared in manuscript.

Place	Date	Hour	Summary of Events and Information	Remarks and references to Appendices
	13th		Church Parade.	
	14th		Specialist training - Range practice - Coys at disposal of O.C. Coys.	
	15th		Battalion with 5th Yorks represented Brigade in Field Firing Scheme at Lucheux Ranges - Gen Mase commanding XLIII Corps was present.	
	16th		Specialist Training - Range Practice	
	17th		Batt moved at 4.0 pm to Chestnut Camp Cojeul	
POIGNEUX	18th		Batt moved at 7.0 a.m. to camp at DOUCHY-LES-AYETTE.	
DOUCHY.LES.AYETTE	19th		Tactical Scheme - Specialist training.	
	20th		Batt Tactical Scheme - Specialist Training - Voluntary Church Parade. The undermentioned men were awarded the Military Medal for operations of April 23rd 20 0022 S.Sgt ROBSON 20 5570 Pte KETCH 20 0340 " BOAL 20 0034 Cpl MERRYWEATHER	
	21st		Batt Training - Brigade scheme in evening - attack on Trenches.	
	22nd		Specialist training.	
	23rd		Batt moved at 10.30. a.m. via ADINFER MONCHY & SOUASTRE to Chestnut Camp POIGNEUX very hot march & several dropped out.	
POIGNEUX	24th		Batt training on ground near BAYON COURT - Reinforcement inspected by B.G.S. in evening	
	25th		Batt Training.	

Army Form C. 2118.

WAR DIARY
or
INTELLIGENCE SUMMARY.
(Erase heading not required.)

Place	Date	Hour	Summary of Events and Information	Remarks and references to Appendices
	26th		Brigade Scheme in the evening Lt Col G.O. SPENCE took over command of 1/5th I Brigade temporarily.	
	27th		Batt Training continued	
	28th			
	29th		Brigade Scheme	
	30th		Coy Training	
	31st		Brigade Contact Aeroplane scheme — Batt inspected at work by G.O.C. Division.	

Lieut Col
Commanding 1/5th Lincoln & Durham Infty

[signature] Mord
Lieut. Col.
Commanding 1st. Line 5th. Bn. Durham L. Infty.

VOLUME 26
MAY 1917
5th Bn Durham L Infty

VOLUME 27
FOR JUNE 1917.

WAR DIARY
1st Bn THE DURHAM LIGHT INFANTRY
or
INTELLIGENCE SUMMARY.
(Erase heading not required.)

Army Form C. 2118.

Instructions regarding War Diaries and Intelligence Summaries are contained in F. S. Regs., Part II. and the Staff Manual respectively. Title pages will be prepared in manuscript.

Vol 24

Place	Date	Hour	Summary of Events and Information	Remarks and references to Appendices
COIGNEUX CHESNUT CAMP	1.6.17		BATTN PARADE - Practice attack - A B & C Coys attack position held by D Coy. Patrols inserted.	
	2.6.17		Officers at 13th (Div) T.G. School. Coys at disposal of O.C. Coys for Inspections. A4 men left unoccupied lines on Ramps.	
	3.6.17		CHURCH PARADE	
	4.6.17		BATT. TRAINING	
			8 O. & N.C.Os went to Lewis Bne & R. BUTTS & WARLENCOURT Lewis Gun butts.	
	5.6.17		BATTN (coy)-S- Specialist training in afternoon. Rings A B & C's & Coys.	
	6.6.17		ADDTNL training - Hot breakfast. Coys at disposal of O.C. Coys. Specialist training in afternoon.	
			A.E. work from 3 p.m. to 5.p.m til 7.30 p.m.	
	7.6.17		BATT. TRAINING to 11 a.m. - Bde Scheme at HERRISSART in afternoon.	
	8.6.17		Coys on B De Stands for musketry and instruction in afternoon. Strength 30/f 22 OR Raised	
	9.6.17		All Coys out and held B D Stands for Instr. Bath inclusive of O. D. & R.	
			A (Cown)	
	10.6.17		CHURCH PARADE. Niat leaves in T.G. 8	
	11.6.17		Running drill. Coys at disposal O.M.Coy. Resumed to Coy. If Bombing & & Co.	
			O.C. Coys Hot Kostras.	
			Running drill. Coys & disposal O.D.C. Coys. Specialist training in B Sections	
	12.6.17		BATTN PARADE Coys at rifle & H.Q. Coys - Specialist Training instructed	
	13.6.17		Coys at disposal of O.C. Coys. Bn. Run of stores - Stores of equip to of Battn	
	14.6.17		BATTN LEWIS L. R. SERTT GON L.A. BRONNETT WORKS W 20A 4 25 25d	

(A7093.) Wt. W12859/M1293 750,000. 11/17. D. D. & L., Ltd. Forms/C2118 84.

Army Form C. 2118.

WAR DIARY
or
INTELLIGENCE SUMMARY.
(Erase heading not required.)

Instructions regarding War Diaries and Intelligence Summaries are contained in F. S. Regs., Part II. and the Staff Manual respectively. Title pages will be prepared in manuscript.

Place	Date	Hour	Summary of Events and Information	Remarks and references to Appendices
BOISLEUX	16.11.17 17.11.17		Coys at disposal of O.C. Coys. Draft in on 1/7th C & Church Parade. Barn inspection & bath at 1.30	
			Position 3 Coys to front line LEFT SUBSECTOR A Coy to RIGHT SUBSECTOR C Coy in SUPPORT D Coy in SUPPORT	
In Front line	18.11.17 - 24.11.17		In trenches. Night of 25-26th R.D.S. of C others took section of front line FONTAINE WOOD	
			Relief then SUNKEN RD [illegible] of FONTAINE Trs from 70 & 2.17 attack on ZERO HOUR 6.20 AM [illegible]	
		6.20 AM	[illegible]	
		8.40 AM	Regt advanced forward [illegible] Must continue [illegible]	
		10 PM	[illegible]	
		10 PM	[illegible]	

WAR DIARY
or
INTELLIGENCE SUMMARY.

Army Form C. 2118.

Place	Date	Hour	Summary of Events and Information	Remarks and references to Appendices
In trenches	26th & 27th		Battn relieved & went back in to support	
	28th & 29th & 30th		At Bray-Lune & Elgers Pot. Carrying parties to trenches. Batt supplied a support trenches - working parties for front line.	

W. Russell Lt Col
R.S.

Army Form C. 2118.

5TH DURHAM L.I.

VOL 25 JULY 1917

WA 25

WAR DIARY
or
INTELLIGENCE SUMMARY.
(Erase heading not required.)

Place	Date	Hour	Summary of Events and Information	Remarks and references to Appendices
Boyelles	2nd	night	Relieved from trenches by 12th Bn. NORTHUMBERLAND FUSILIERS and moved back to BOYELLES.	
"	3rd		Coys at disposal of O.C. Coys for Coy training. Latest drafts inspected by Commanding Officer.	
Neuville Vitasse	4th		Moved from BOYELLES to NEUVILLE VITASSE.	
"	5th		Battalion Parade. Bayonet fighting course for selected officers & N.C.O's. Musical Inspection.	
"	6th		Early morning Parade. Coys at disposal of O.C. Coys for training. Baths at NEUVILLE VITASSE allotted to Battn.	
"	7th		Early morning Parade. Battn. Parade in morning.	
"	8th		Church Parade. Baths allotted to Battn. Range allotted to Coys.	
"	9th		Coys at disposal of O.C. Coys when not bathing. Working parties detailed.	
Tunnel	10th		Battn. moved to trenches and relieved 5th Bn. NTHN. FUSILIERS on the front line. Disposition as follows:- A & B Coys in front line C Coy in support D Coy in reserve Battn moved off at 4.15 p.m.	

Army Form C. 2118.

WAR DIARY
or
INTELLIGENCE SUMMARY.
(Erase heading not required.)

Instructions regarding War Diaries and Intelligence Summaries are contained in F. S. Regs., Part II. and the Staff Manual respectively. Title pages will be prepared in manuscript.

Place	Date	Hour	Summary of Events and Information	Remarks and references to Appendices
Trenches	11/12		In Trenches	
"	12/13	night	Inter-Bn relief. "A" Coy relieved "C" Coy. "B" Coy relieved "D" Coy. "A" Coy moved back into support. "B" Coy into reserve.	
"	13/16		In Trenches.	
"	16/17	night	Battn. relieved by 4 Yorks Regt and moved back into support. Hdqt. Bn. in THE NEST. Coys in EGRET TRENCH and LOOP and ALBATROSS TRENCH.	
"	17/20		Battn. supplied working parties daily for the TUNNELLING COY RE and worked on improving the C.T'S and trenches in Bn area.	
"	21/ot		Battn. relieved 5th YORKS REGT on LEFT SECTOR of front line "A" COY right front line "B" COY left front line "C" COY CUCKOO TRENCH support "D" COY MALLARD TRENCH reserve.	
"	21/24		In Trenches	
"	24/25		Inter Bn relief. "C" Coy relieved "A" Coy. "D" Coy relieved "B" Coy.	
"	25/26		In Trenches	
"	26th	night	Raid by 1 Officer and 20 O.R. on Boche Lines.	
"	27th		Relieved by 5th BORDER REGT. Moved back to Camp at NEUVILLE VITASSE	

Army Form C. 2118

WAR DIARY
or
INTELLIGENCE SUMMARY

VOLUME 28
JULY

(Erase heading not required.)

Place	Date	Hour	Summary of Events and Information	Remarks and references to Appendices
Merville Area	28th		Coys at disposal of O.C. Coys for re-fitting and inspections. Rifle inspection by Armourer Sgt. Raiding Party inspected by B.G.C.	
"	29th		Church Parade and Bath.	
"	30th		Early Morning Parade. Coys at disposal of O.C. Coys for Training. Range allotted to bgn. Coys practical Bayonet fighting.	
"	31st		Early Morning Parade. Coy training. Specialist classes.	

[signature]
Lieut. Col.
Commanding 1st Line 5th Bn. Durham L. Infy.

WAR DIARY

VOLUME 29.

5th Bn DURHAM LIGHT INF.

AUGUST 1917

Vol 26

Army Form C. 2118.

Place	Date	Hour	Summary of Events and Information	Remarks and references to Appendices
NEUVILLE VITASSE	1st		Coys at disposal of OC Coys. Box Respirators inspection. Supper & working parties.	
	2		Went to trenches by OC Coys prior to taking over.	
	3		Boys at disposal of OC Coys. Specialist training. Relieved Bath at Neuville Vitasse for Battn.	
	4		Relieved 7th Bn Northumberland Fusiliers in Support trenches. Disposition "B" Coy relieved B Coy 7th NF. "C" " " C " " " "D" " " D " " " Between C & D Coys First Coy moved off at 7.15 p.m. Remainder at 10 minutes interval.	
TRENCHES	5/20		In trenches. 7th Bn. relieved in front line by 9th DLI. OC Coys for Fraganzalin and inspection on Bath at disposal of OC Coys.	
NEUVILLE VITASSE	21		Bath at disposal of OC Coys. Specialist training. Cooperation by DGC 150th Bgde. Ranges allocated to 4 Companies. Specialist training.	
	22/23		Coys at disposal of OC Coys.	
	24		Cooperation by DGC of OC Coys.	
	25		Boys at disposal of OC Coys.	
	26		Church Parades.	
	27		Coys at disposal of OC Coys. Specialist training. Working parties supplied for RE. Reorganisation of Company football.	
BDE RESERVE	28		Reviewed at Northumberland medals to Batt. Prog. winners of Coast Competition. A Coy in Sacki Trench & Grey St, B Coy in Croisilles Trench in Edgar at Henin Camp.	
	29/31		Training continued at Henin Camp.	

W. Greer
Lieut. Col.
Commanding 1st Line 5th. Bn. Durham L. Infty.

Volume 29
August
1917

Vol. 30 SEPTEMBER 1917

Army Form C. 2118.

WAR DIARY
5th Bn DURHAM LIGHT INFANTRY
INTELLIGENCE SUMMARY

(Erase heading not required.)

Instructions regarding War Diaries and Intelligence Summaries are contained in F. S. Regs., Part II. and the Staff Manual respectively. Title pages will be prepared in manuscript.

Place	Date	Hour	Summary of Events and Information	Remarks and references to Appendices
TRENCHES	1st		Relieved 4th E. Yorks Regt in front line trenches of RIGHT SUBSECTION: RIGHT SECTION. Disposition. A Coy, BUSH and BUSH TRENCHES and TODD. B Coy (Centre) in SNIPE, SWIFT and WOOD TRENCHES. C Coy (Left) SWIFT TR. D Coy (in Reserve) in SUNKEN ROAD.	
Bde Reserve.	5.		Relieved by 4th Bn YORKS REGT. and moved to Brigade Reserve. MENIN CAMP. Distribution HQ. A & B Coys. MENIN CAMP. D Coy in ZARIES COURT. C Coy in CONCRETE TR. Training continued at MENIN CAMP.	
TRENCHES.	9.		Relieved 4th Bn YORKS REGT in front line. Distribution. D Coy (R.S./O) BUSH, TODD & BROWN TRS. B Coy (Centre) SNIPE, WOOD and SWIFT TR. C Coy (Lft) in SWIFT TR. A Coy (Reserve) in SUNKEN R.D.	
	13.		Relieved in trenches by 6th Bn D.L.I. and moved back to Destroyed Reserve in NORTHUMBERLAND LINES.	
NORTHUMBERLAND LINES.	15.		4 Officers & 20 O.R. moved to HINDENBURG LINE for work under R.E. Barks.	
do	14/16		Training. Working Parties. Church Parade.	
do	17.		Divis'l HQ (Parties returned from HINDENBURG LINE. A & B Coys detachments at HINDENBURG LINE returned by C & D Coys under Capt A.B. Kirk.	
do	19/20		Training & Working parties continued.	
do	21.		Relieved 9th Bn. N.F. in SUPPORT in LEFT SUBSECTION. Distribution. A Coy in MORTIERS. B Coy in DURHAM TR. C Coy in LION, HUN SAP & EGYPT TR. D Coy Reserve in MORTIERS.	
	25.		Relieved the 4th EAST YORKS REGT in front line. Distribution. A Coy RIGHT SECTION. B Coy SUPPORT (BISON) MORT TR. C Coy RESERVE (BISON).	
TRENCHES	28/29		In front line trenches.	
	29		Relieved by 4th EAST YORKS REGT and moved to Bde Reserve at HAPPLES VITLASSE	
do	30.		Retting and change of O.	

A.Rawing Major
for Lieut. Col.
Commanding 1st. Line 5th. Bn. Durham L. Infty.

VOLUME 31
OCTOBER 1917

5 Bn DURHAM LIGHT INFANTRY

WAR DIARY
INTELLIGENCE SUMMARY.

(Erase heading not required.)

Army Form C. 2118.

VOLUME 31
OCTOBER 1917

Vol 28

Place	Date	Hour	Summary of Events and Information	Remarks and references to Appendices
NEUVILLE VITASSE	1st		Lt. Col. Y. L. Spence D.S.O. in command of 150th Infantry Brigade. Major J. L. Farmer commanding 5th D.L.I.	
	3rd		Coy Training and range firing carried out. Battalion moved to Trenches during day and relieved 4th East Yorks Regt. on right sub-section of left section. Distribution of Coys was as under:- A Coy Reserve in BISON and supplied anti-raiding platoon B " Right front line C " Left " " D " Res (2 platoons) support in APE TRENCH	
TRENCHES	4th		The distribution was revised during the day, new posts being formed and a certain portion of the old front line being abandoned. A Coy right front line B " centre " C " the front line D " support	
do.	5th		Battn. relieved by 9th Royal Scots 51st Div. After relief it entrained at HENIN and trained SWINDON and was billeted for the night at NORTHUMBERLAND LINES. The relief was complete by 2.30 p.m. and passed off well. The tour was quiet, work done viewing round new posts and abandoned portion of line. Casualties 1 N.C.O.	

Army Form C. 2118.

WAR DIARY
or
INTELLIGENCE SUMMARY.
(Erase heading not required.)

VOLUME 31
OCTOBER 1917

Instructions regarding War Diaries and Intelligence Summaries are contained in F.S. Regs., Part II. and the Staff Manual respectively. Title pages will be prepared in manuscript.

Place	Date	Hour	Summary of Events and Information	Remarks and references to Appendices
	6th		Battalion moved at 11.30 a.m. by road to ACHIET-LE-PETIT via BOYELLES and ACHIET-LE-GRAND. Route was very rough, weather was bad and going heavy but Batn marched well and no one fell out.	
ACHIET-LE-PETIT	7th		At HENHAM CAMP, ACHIET-LE-PETIT. Batn settled in, held inspections and tried to get huts comfortable into some semblance of order. Weather appallingly bad. Lecture on use of pigeons in evening.	
do.	8th		Worked enforced and training commenced. Platoon and Coy work each morning, bayonet training in afternoon followed by a lecture at 6 p.m. on by 2nd Lt Banks, 9th Royal Scots, on recent fighting in Ypres district. Hours of work 9 a.m. - 12 noon. 1 p.m. - 3 p.m.	
do.	9th		Close order and physical training carried out, voluntary training compulsory. In the evening all lectured to all officers and it arranged at 8 p.m. by 3rd Lydd played 16th D.L.I. on Battn ground and ended by a goal to nil by of Blumer signed Battn temporarily attached to the 2nd Lyon Royer went to hospital sick.	
do.	10th		Training as above. Lecture to N.C.Os by O.C. to Officers by 2nd Lt Eng, L. of 70 men from 7th D.C.L.I attached to us. Capt J. D. Webb proceeded to England for 7 months duty to England for 6 months.	
do.	11th		Training as above. Lecture to Officers by 2nd Lt Banks 9th Royal Scots on Platoon training. Brigade Conference at Brigade.	

WAR DIARY
or
INTELLIGENCE SUMMARY.
(Erase heading not required.)

Army Form C. 2118.

VOLUME 31
OCTOBER 1917

Place	Date	Hour	Summary of Events and Information	Remarks and references to Appendices
ACHIET-LE-PETIT	12th		Brigade tactical scheme cancelled owing to weather. Coys went marched and short Batn. parade. Majors Baines lectured to officers on consolidation. Afternoon, bathing.	
do	13th		Turning as above. Batn. had use of 200 yds range and bathing.	
do	14th		Church Parade. Bathing and range work.	
do	15th		Batn. Parade 9.0 a.m. - 11.0 a.m. followed by Field Firing on range by Platoons. Early stand to and preparations made for move.	
do	16th		Lt. Col. G. W. Pierce D.S.O. re-assumed command of Batn. Battn. paraded for move on following day. Final of football competition played. E Coy v. D Coy. E Coy won by 2 goals to nil.	
do	17th		Batn. less "A" Coy left ACHIET CAMP and marched to MIRAUMONT and entrained at 12 noon. Nothing eventful happened on the journey and Batn. detrained at BAVINCOURT at 9.0 p.m. Tea was given to the men, guides etc went on ahead and Batn. moved off at 11.0 p.m. for RUBROUCK via ZUTYPEEN & NORDPEEN arriving about 2.30 a.m. after a wearyful about 9 miles. The night was extraordinarily black and we frequently had to find our way, the guides were packed up, our guides and Coys marched off to Billets on farms which were very scattered.	
RUBROUCK	18th		At RUBROUCK Batn. rested. Lt. Col. A. M. Hamelen assumed the Batn. and took over command of "B" Coy.	
	19th		B.G.O. conference cancelled. Coy training at Billets and short route march	

Army Form C. 2118.

WAR DIARY
or
INTELLIGENCE SUMMARY.

VOLUME 31
OCTOBER 1917

(Erase heading not required.)

Instructions regarding War Diaries and Intelligence Summaries are contained in F. S. Regs., Part II. and the Staff Manual respectively. Title pages will be prepared in manuscript.

Place	Date	Hour	Summary of Events and Information	Remarks and references to Appendices
RUBROUCK	20th		Day training as before. O.I.C. 150 & H/g Bde addressed all officers at Battn. H.Qrs. Coys prepared for move.	
do	21st		Battn moved from RUBROUCK at 10.0 a.m. via ARNEKE to LEDRINGHEM arriving 12 noon and were billeted in village and surrounding area.	
LEDRINGHEM	22nd		Battn left LEDRINGHEM at 7.15 a.m. and marched to PROVEN arriving at 2.15 p.m. where two were killed at POODLE CAMP. March route WERMOLDT and HOUTKERQUE. 103 men of the Battn came by train from WERMOLDT.	
PROVEN	23rd		At POODLE CAMP PROVEN Inspections and preparing for move.	
do	24th		Moved from POODLE CAMP to SUTTON CAMP 3 km. N.W. of POPERINGHE. Left at 9.15 a.m. arrived at 10.0 a.m. In afternoon inter platoon football competition was held.	
	25th		Battn less 105 men who remained behind at SUTTON CAMP moved near POPERINGHE to ROUSSEL FARM camp near ELVERDINGHE. Battn prepared for going into action. E.O.'s Intelligence Officer reconnoitred forward routes. Officers conference in evening.	
	26th		Battn at ROUSSEL CAMP preparing for trenches.	
	27th		Battn moved at 5.0 a.m. via ELVERDINGHE and BOESINGHE to MARSOUIN FARM and at dusk moved again to the support area near the remains of PASCAL FARM (1½ miles N.N.E. LANGEMARK ¼ mile the YPRES - STADEN railway) which suffered into a platoon of D COY on the way up and caused a considerable number of casualties.	

Army Form C. 2118.

WAR DIARY
or
INTELLIGENCE SUMMARY.
(Erase heading not required.)

Instructions regarding War Diaries and Intelligence Summaries are contained in F. S. Regs., Part II. and the Staff Manual respectively. Title pages will be prepared in manuscript.

Place	Date	Hour	Summary of Events and Information	Remarks and references to Appendices
	28th		Battn still at PASCAL FARM in support. Hostile shelling severe, especially so the only cover available was holes torn on three feet deep scratched in the mud.	
	29th		Battn still in support at PASCAL FARM.	
	30th		do do	
	31st		3rd Batt remaining in support. 4th East Yorks attacked at do. During the evening German aeroplanes dropped a lot of bombs round ELVERDINGHE and three of our men were wounded.	

W. Harris Major
Comdg. 5th Battn 19.2.L

WAR DIARY or INTELLIGENCE SUMMARY

5th DURHAM L.I.
VOLUME 32
NOVEMBER 1917

Army Form C. 2118

(Erase heading not required.)

Place	Date	Hour	Summary of Events and Information	Remarks and references to Appendices
	1st	—	Battn in trenches at PASCAL FARM relieved at 8.0 p.m. by 5th BORDER REGT and proceeded into camp at HULL FARM near BOESINGHE. The march down was quiet and there were no casualties. The march down was quiet and there were no casualties for the tour were Officers 2 wounded {2nd Lt Stockdale / 2nd Lt Barker O.R.s Killed 13 Wounded 46 Missing 5 Gassed Sick Shell shock } 59	
	2nd	—	At HULL FARM. Coys at disposal of O.C. Coys for inspections etc	
	3rd	—	Coys at disposal of O/Coys for reorganization, bathing etc. working party of 50 men supplied to 7th Field Coy R.E. for walk over HULLFARM camp. Lt Gland R.G.E. revisited the Bn.	
	4th	—	Coys at disposal of O.C. Coys. working party of 50 men supplied to 7th Coy R.E. Football played in afternoon. 2 Officers joined the Bn Lieut Lobb and Lobb his leg Lieut v Dr. Paterson re-joined Battn after being absent sick.	
HULL CAMP	5th		HULL CAMP. Coys at disposal of O.C. Coys. Working parties of 2 & 2 under R.E.	
	6th 7th		At HULL CAMP as before	

WAR DIARY or **INTELLIGENCE SUMMARY**
(Erase heading not required.)

Army Form C. 2118

3rd DURHAM L.I.
VOLUME 32
NOVEMBER 1917

Place	Date	Hour	Summary of Events and Information	Remarks and references to Appendices
	9th		Working parties as before. Coys prepared for move. Lieut Morrison M.C. returned from Comdts leave night of 8/9th.	
	10th		Batln less transport moved by road to CARIBOU CAMP near POPERINGHE, via ELVERDINGHE. Left HULL CAMP 10.0 a.m. arrived 11.0 p.m. Going was bad and the column was held up repeatedly by traffic. Incidentally at CARIBOU had Transport left at 6.0 a.m. and moved to BUYSCHEURE and from there on morning of 11th to NORTLEULINGHAM near WATTEN. Capt. P. Wood D.S.O. went ahead the billet the Batln.	
	11th		Batln left CARIBOU CAMP at 9.0 a.m. and marched to entraining station at "INTERNATIONAL CORNER" near EYNHOUCK. 150 O.R.s & Batln. Hdqrs and ourselves entrained and left at 11.30 a.m. Detrained at WATTEN at 3.30 p.m. Cookers met us 1 km. from station and men were given hot tea. After they Batln marched to billeting area, NORTLEULINGHEN. Billets on the whole were good and comfortable.	
	12th		Coys at disposal of O.C.Coys for cleaning up and re-organizing. Lieut. Col. Offence D.S.O. left for a month leave in England. Major T.L. Reiner assumed command of Batln. Capt. P. Wood D.S.O. becomes 2nd in command and Lieut Major Morrison N.C. takes over command of "C" COY.	

WAR DIARY or INTELLIGENCE SUMMARY

5th DURHAM L.I.
VOLUME 32
NOVEMBER 1917

Army Form C. 2118

Place	Date	Hour	Summary of Events and Information	Remarks and references to Appendices
	13th		Coys at disposal of O.C. Coys for re-organizing and training. Officers Conference in evening.	
	14th		Platoon training and musketry on 30 yds range. Coy commanded new 500 yds range. Coy canteen, cinema, and football commenced. Talent Jollity gave concert at 7.30 p.m. in Church Army Hut.	
	15th		Battn fired 2 musketry practices at 200 yds and 500 yds respectively at "B" range P.H.B. under Brigade arrangements. Shooting very poor too low throughout the day. Coy light weapons training.	
	16th		Coy training musketry and bathing.	
	17th		"A" Coy Training, "B" Coy acting as an attacking force in conjunction with tactical scheme of 50 yards of 5 x B Coys battery. General Trenus Coys training under XVIII Corps orders the Battn at work.	
	18th		Church Parade and Sports.	
	19th		Battn Training attack across open practised. Battn moved out to TOURNEHAM as advance guard, then attacked across towards NORTLEULINGHAM windmill.	
	20th		Coy training and musketry. B.G.C. held conference of all Officers at the Mess at 6.10 p.m., subject "organization."	

Army Form C. 2118

WAR DIARY
or
INTELLIGENCE SUMMARY
(Erase heading not required.)

5th DURHAM L.I.
VOLUME 32
NOVEMBER 1917

Place	Date	Hour	Summary of Events and Information	Remarks and references to Appendices
	21st		Battalion Musketry under Brigade arrangements commenced 9 a.m. fired until 3.0 p.m. Conference of C.O's with reference to Bole scheme.	
	22nd		Coy training. W. and officers rec'd ground for Brigade defence scheme coming off tomorrow. Capt J. Bloomer promoted to substantive Major. 2nd Lieut J. Grenville Jones appointed G.M. 3, 50th Div. with temporary rank of Captain. Capt W.H. Robson appointed Staff.	
	23rd		Brigade Exercise. 5th D.L.I. Left 105th Infy Bde 35th Div. Left W.H. Robson appointed Staff Capt left 5th Yorks on left attached below from MENTQUE towards the CALAIS–ST OMER road. Commenced 9 a.m. finished 1.0 p.m. followed by conference at which Divisional General was present.	
	24th		Transport inspected by B.G.C. Coy training continued.	
	25th		Brigade Church Parade. In afternoon 5th D.L.I. played 2 N.F's at HOGUE. Result 2 N.F's 2 goals 5th D.L.I. 1 goal, and in the evening the officer party known as "HARTY MORRISONS MERRY MASCOTS" gave a concert to the men.	
	26th		Battalion parade & inspection. Boys at disposal of troops afterwards.	
	27th		Brigade Musketry owing to weather was cancelled. Boys at disposal of officers.	

Army Form C. 2118

WAR DIARY
or
INTELLIGENCE SUMMARY

(Erase heading not required.)

5TH DURHAM. L.I.
VOLUME 32
NOVEMBER 1917.

Instructions regarding War Diaries and Intelligence Summaries are contained in F.S. Regs., Part II. and the Staff Manual respectively. Title Pages will be prepared in manuscript.

Place	Date	Hour	Summary of Events and Information	Remarks and references to Appendices
	28d	-	Command of Battn assumed by Capt P. Wood. D.S.O. from Major H.L. Raimes attending Senior Officers Course at BOULEZELE. Coy training carried out Officers riding class etc.	
	29d		Coy training. Forward Guns allotted to "A" & "B" Coys. Find an afternoon in Brigade Range. B & C Coys bathed in afternoon. 2nd Lt Grant awarded M.C. for good work while in charge of Brigade Carrying Party. Sjt Pelman of Transport Section awarded M.M for good work near LANGEMARCK.	
	30d		Coy training and route march, extensive digging and carrying practice.	

P.Wood Capt.
Lieut. Col.
Commanding 1st. Line 5th. Bn. Durham L. Infty.

5th Bn. Durham L.I.

WAR DIARY
or
INTELLIGENCE SUMMARY.

Army Form C. 2118.
VOLUME 33
DECEMBER 1917

Vol 30

Place	Date	Hour	Summary of Events and Information	Remarks and references to Appendices
NORTLEULINGHAM	1st		Coy. Training "A" & "D" Coys allotted Bullet & Bayonet Course. "B" & "C" Coys allotted "B" Range. Owing to weather only 1 practise was fired. Sergts gave a concert in the evening.	
	2nd		Batt'n relieved 7th N.F's in SERQUES area, moved from NORTLEULINGHAM at 10.0 a.m. arrived new area at 12 noon. Billets good, reconnaissance small training area practically nil. O & Coys conference at night.	
SERQUES	3rd	9.0 a.m – 11.0 a.m	Platoon & Coy training	
		11.15 a.m – 1.0 p.m	Route March of the whole Batt'n not running	
		1.0 p.m	Competition between for Divisional Cross Country Championship in which 5th D.L.I represented the 150th Brigade.	
	4th		All officers and platoon Sgts. attended lecture on co-operation at MEULLE by Lieut Col. Hewy. D.S.O. Commanding VIII Loyal North Lancashire Remainder of Batt'n carried out marked under Coy & Pl'n Officers D.S.O	
	5th		Coy & platoon training, expert wiring, rifle grenade firing. Coy night operations	
	6th		Brigade Musketry on "B" Range. Major Barnes DSO M.L.S.A. & Lieut Green shot syd at the tiles	

WAR DIARY or INTELLIGENCE SUMMARY

Army Form C. 2118.

VOLUME 33   DECEMBER 1917

(Erase heading not required.)

Place	Date	Hour	Summary of Events and Information	Remarks and references to Appendices
SERQUES	7th	—	Platoon and Coy training when not installing. Coys of Personnel short now of 15 offrs & 15 oth ranks of completion of the Units war est. Drafts of 78 men arrived	
	8th		Coy & platoon training	
	9th		Church Parade	
BRANDHOEK	10th		Left SERQUES at 6.15 a.m & entrained at WATTEN. Detrained about noon at BRANDHOEK and marched to hutments known as TORONTO CAMP.	
TRENCHES	11th		Entrained at BRANDHOEK at 6.0 p.m. Detrained at YPRES and marched on the duck walk & menin Road to POTIZE, where we relieved the 10th Royal Fusiliers (33rd Div.) In the afternoon and evening we moved up to the close support area on the slopes of the PASSCHENDAELE RIDGE & relieved the 4th Suffolk Regt (33rd Div.)	
	12th		Relieved the left front Baton, & things in front of PASSCHENDAEL village the 1st East Yorks being on our right and the 14th Div on our left. A & B Coys were in the front line each with Coy HQrs and a reserve platoon in cellars or dug outs in the village and the remainder on foot. C Coy was in support near the ridge road and D Coy in reserve near Baton Wood.	

WAR DIARY or INTELLIGENCE SUMMARY

Army Form C. 2118.

VOLUME 33
DECEMBER 1917.

Place	Date	Hour	Summary of Events and Information	Remarks and references to Appendices
TRENCHES	13th		D" Coy moved forward to HAALEN SPUR and dug themselves in small holes. The situation they changed over with a Coy of the 1st Borderers and took up a position on the CREST FARM spur.	
POTIZZE	16th		We were relieved by the 5th N.F's and went down to POTIZE. The turn was rather a trying one as the shelling was heavy. Getting rations to the front line was difficult owing to the saltness + the rations parties constantly lost their way. Our casualties from shell fire was total casualties were 7 killed, 25 wounded and 16 went down sick. During the tour enemy aeroplanes were very active and flew so low over our heads that on one case the observer could be seen trying to locate the exact position of our posts. They also used their machine guns freely as our boys observed when he attempted to perform all efforts of nature outside the hill for move as Button H Dos. On our arrival at POTIZZE, Lt Col G. Spence DSO having returned from leave, resumed command of the Batten	
BRANDHOEK	17th		Moved by motor bus to ERIE CAMP near BRANDHOEK and went into Divisional Reserve	

WAR DIARY or INTELLIGENCE SUMMARY

Army Form C. 2118.
VOLUME 33
DECEMBER 1917

Place	Date	Hour	Summary of Events and Information	Remarks and references to Appendices
BRANDHOEK	18th		Bay Commanders' Conference at Brigade H.Q.	
	19th		C.O. inspected B. Y. + D. Coys.	
	20th		C.O. inspected A. Coy. Short Coy route marches	
	21st		Marched through VLAMERTINGHE and YPRES to POTIJZE + became the working battalion of the Brigade in place of the 4th Yorks.	
POTIJZE	22nd to 31st		We lived at POTIJZE in ALNWICK CAMP, the accommodation being about empty tents. From 200 to 250 men went out each day carrying. Most of the parties started about 5.0 a.m. or 6.0 a.m. but were back by 10.0 a.m. to 12 noon. The work was on the area east + north east of FREZENBERG and consisted of carrying and dumping "duck boards" for improving the approaches to the PASSCHENDAEL area. We also working an artillery track of stepping. A lot of work was done on the camp. Two wash huts were put up + most of the tents surrounded by sandbag bombs. Roads into the camp + new bone standings were also made. Christmas Day was celebrated by giving the men about 30 lbs. of pork for their dinner. They also had P.I. government issue of pudding + followers.	

Lieut. Col.
Commanding 1st. Line 5th. Bn. Durham L. Infty.

5TH DURHAM L.I. VOLUME 34 JANY. 1918

Army Form C. 2118.

WAR DIARY
or
INTELLIGENCE SUMMARY
(Erase heading not required.)

Place	Date	Hour	Summary of Events and Information	Remarks and references to Appendices
POTIJZE	1st/2nd		Working parties of about 230 men in all supplied to R.E. commencing work about 5:30 a.m.	
do	2nd		Batt'n moved from ALNWICK CAMP, POTIJZE to No 3 Billeting Area WINEZEELE leaving the Square YPRES by buses at 10.30 a.m. and arriving at WINEZEELE 12.30 p.m. Billets very scattered.	
WINEZEELE	3rd		Muster Parade 7.45 a.m. Instructions and re-organizing Battalion. Alarm Post on STEENVOORDE – WINEZEELE ROAD at K.36.c.3.2.	
do	6th		Church Parades. B.G's at Steenvoorde, R.C's at L/Sgt Biles.	
do	7th		Men to Parade 7.45 a.m. Batt. Inspection by Brigadier Gen'l.	
do	8th		Muster Parade 7.45 a.m. Commanding Officers inspection, by as follows:— D. Coy. 9.30 a.m. Y. Coy. 10.30 a.m. Z. Coy. 11.30 a.m. H.Q.'s Wheel carts Reg'l Coys. Trans'p'rt 1 p.m.	
do	9th		Muster Parade 7.45 a.m. Training as before. Range allotted to "A" & "B" Coy's Lewis Gun Class. Report on Transport 5th D.L.I. Transport and bad turned out on the Divison on move from Dozys to Winizeele	

Army Form C. 2118.

WAR DIARY
or
INTELLIGENCE SUMMARY.
(Erase heading not required.)

VOLUME 34
JAN. 1918

Place	Date	Hour	Summary of Events and Information	Remarks and references to Appendices
WINEZEELE	10		Winter Parade 7.45am. Coy Training as before. Lewis Gun Class and Stretcher Bearers training.	
do	11		Winter Parade 7.45am. Coy Training as before. L.G. expected to do Head and Billets Inspected to P.M.D boys	
do	12		Winter Parade 7.45am Coy Training and Musketry as before.	
do	13		Voluntary C. of E. Parade at Wenyde. 6ys at Baths.	
do	14		Training enlivened with by snow. Lecture by Lieut Powers during afternoon for Officers & N.C.O's on "Looking and Identifying an aeroplane".	
do	15		Coy Training. 1 Officer and 3 O.Rs went off to New Drive.	
do	16		Battalion entrained from GODEWAERSVELDE at 2.0 p.m and detrained at WIZERNES (near St Omer) at 4.30 p.m. Marched through HALLINES and SETQUE to our billets at QUELMES.	
QUELMES	17		Very bad weather. Platoons employed on jobs in their billets.	
do	18		Signallers & Scouts under Specialist Officers. Coys sent on march.	

Army Form C. 2118.

WAR DIARY
or
INTELLIGENCE SUMMARY.
(Erase heading not required.)

VOLUME 34
JAN'Y 1915

Instructions regarding War Diaries and Intelligence Summaries are contained in F. S. Regs., Part II. and the Staff Manual respectively. Title pages will be prepared in manuscript.

Place	Date	Hour	Summary of Events and Information	Remarks and references to Appendices
QUELMES	19th		Signallers & Scouts under Specialist Officers. Coy Training.	
do	20th		Church Parade at 9 AM. C.O. Out at LEULINGHAM. Coys at Baths. Y.M.S. 1 Div. employed Transport.	
do	21st			
do	22nd		Firing on ¼" range most of the day. The first 5 practises out of the 9 in Part II Y.M.S.	
do	23rd		Bat'n route march via TATINGHEM and WIZQUES.	
do	24th		Bat'n Drill. Witnessed demonstration of efficiency of new officers at various heights. Lt Col G.A.Hope D.S.O. returned from Base Bat'n and resumed command of the Bat'n.	
do	25th		On ¼" range. Completed Part II.	
do	26th		Coy Training. C.O. tested several of the new officers in Coy Drill	
do	27th		Church Parade at LEULINGHAM with 2nd East Yorks. An advance party of Officers and O.R's proceeded to YPRES.	
do	28		Bat'n marched to WIZERNES and entrained there. Detrained at YPRES and took over a collection of cellars in the vicinity of the old Infantry Barracks from the 5th N.F's	

Army Form C. 2118.

WAR DIARY
or
INTELLIGENCE SUMMARY.
(Erase heading not required.)

VOLUME
JAN 1918

Instructions regarding War Diaries and Intelligence Summaries are contained in F. S. Regs., Part II. and the Staff Manual respectively. Title pages will be prepared in manuscript.

Place	Date	Hour	Summary of Events and Information	Remarks and references to Appendices
YPRES	29/30th		Batts. remained at YPRES as part of the Brigade in support. Working and carrying Parties were supplied.	

G. W. Laun
Lieut. Col.
Commanding 1st Line 5th Bn. Durham L. Infty.

50

1/5 Durham L I

Vol IX

50

1/5 Durham L.D.
Vol VIII

www.ingramcontent.com/pod-product-compliance
Lightning Source LLC
Chambersburg PA
CBHW081358160426
43193CB00013B/2061